STRETCH OUT YOUR HAND

The Journey in Faith for Those Seeking to Know More About the Catholic Church

Kenneth Payne

Illustrated by
Chris Costello

UPFRONT PUBLISHING
LEICESTERSHIRE

STRETCH OUT YOUR HAND

ISBN 1-84426-254-5

First Published 1998 by
MINERVA PRESS

Second Edition 2003 by
UPFRONT PUBLISHING
Leicestershire

Printed by Lightning Source

STRETCH OUT YOUR HAND

The Journey in Faith for Those Seeking to Know More About the Catholic Church

All proceeds from this book will go to The Missionaries of the Poor in Jamaica, India, the Philippines, Haiti and Uganda.

Registered Charity No. 1048926
Account No. 07140041
Lloyds Bank
64 Harborough Road
Kingsthorpe
Northampton NN2 7SM

To my father, John Henry Payne, to whom I owe so much; John Danford, whose idea it was; Judith Bentley and Philip and Sally Nash, who have helped by their advice and encouragement; Sue (Woo) Beck, who had the arduous task of deciphering my scrawl and setting it all up on the word processor; Chris Costello, for the meaningful and humorous illustrations; Louise Sheppard and Pat Brierley, for correcting the proofs; the late Michael Richards, for his most helpful comments and corrections; and finally, to the editor at Minerva Press, for the careful and useful editing.

Thank you.

Acknowledgements

Extracts taken from *The New Jerusalem Bible*, published and copyright 1985 by Darton Longman and Todd Ltd and Doubleday & Co. Inc., and used by permission of the publishers.

Quotations from Anthony de Mello's books reproduced by permission of Gujarat Sahitya Prakash, Publishers and Booksellers, India.

PEANUTS cartoon: Copyright (1978) United Feature Syndicate, Inc. Reproduced by permission.

Diagnosis of Man by Kenneth Walker, Jonathan Cape, 1942. Reproduced by permission of Random House UK Ltd.

'I am the bread of life' by David Konstant and 'The Spirit lives to set us free' by Damian Lundy. Copyright by Kevin Mayhew Ltd. Used by permission from *Hymns Old and New*, Licence No. 791172JR.

Quotation from H.V. Morton, Methuen. Reproduced by permission of Random House UK Ltd.

The Resurrection of Jesus by Gerald O'Collins, SJ (Do.561). Reproduced by permission of the Catholic Truth Society.

Occasional Sermons of Ronald A. Knox: On Divine Providence by Ronald Knox, Burns & Oates, 1960. Reproduced by permission of Burns & Oates.

Extract from Rabbi Lionel Blue reproduced by permission of Sheil Land Associates Ltd. Copyright Lionel Blue.

Quotation from Douglas Woodruffe in *The Tablet.* Reproduced by permission of The Tablet Publishing Co. Ltd.

Man's Search for Meaning by Viktor Frankl. Reproduced by permission of Hodder and Stoughton Limited.

Prayer from *The Divine Milieu (Le Milieu divin)* by Pierre Teilhard de Chardin, Editions du Seuil, 1957. Reproduced by permission.

Statement by Cardinal Hume in *Briefing*, 1987. Reproduced by permission of the Catholic Media Office.

Science and Christ by Pierre Teilhard de Chardin, Editions du Seuil, 1968. Reproduced by permission.

Faith and Contemplation by René Voillaume, 1974, Darton Longman and Todd Ltd. Reproduced by permission.

The Little Prince by de Saint Exupery, William Heinemann. Reproduced by permission of Reed Consumer Books Ltd.

A Journey in Faith by Raymond Kemp, William H. Sadlier, Inc. Reproduced by permission of William H. Sadlier, Inc.

The Catechism of the Catholic Church Geoffrey Chapman (an imprint of Cassell plc).

The Documents of Vatican II, Walter M. Abbott (ed.) Geoffrey Chapman (an imprint of Cassell plc).

The English Translation of the Gloria and Nicene Creed by the International Consultation on English texts

About the Author

The author, a Catholic priest and a convert himself, has had many years of experience in leading groups of people journeying towards reception into the Catholic Church, as well as others who have lost touch with the Christianity of their upbringing. His pastoral work has been mainly in the Northampton diocese, in Bedford, Aylesbury and Northampton, with a spell as chaplain to the RAF in both England and Cyprus.

He is at present parish priest in Little Chalfont, Bucks., and continues to be involved with married couples' groups (Teams of Our Lady) and the support of the homeless and destitute in different parts of the world (Missionaries of the Poor Supporters Association).

Introduction

This book is an attempt to set down the fruits of many years of experience in passing on 'the faith' to very mixed groups of non-Catholics and to those who have been away from the Church for a while. It is in no way a work of theology, but is designed to be readable and practical and to offer some concrete teaching. It can be used as a guide for catechist, sponsor, priest or leader of a group, but, at the same time, I hope it will be especially useful as a book to be perused at home by the individual being instructed.

Frequently, programmes designed for those seeking to know more about the Catholic Church are tarnished by the use of unfamiliar terminology (RCIA, catechumens, mystagogy and so on). I have tried to avoid this, as far as possible, by setting out the whole programme in terms of an extended meal:

APPETISER	⇨	General introductory stage
MAIN COURSE	⇨	Instructional stage
DESSERT	⇨	Lenten spiritual lead-up to Easter
COFFEE	⇨	Digesting it all at Eastertide

The leader of the group would be well advised to read the excellent 'Introduction' to the RCIA, together with the actual rites to be used, always bearing in mind that 'adaptation' to the particular parish or group situation is of paramount importance.

The order of topics will be seen to vary from other comparable presentations. The early Church, and indeed that which has existed throughout the ages, centred its preaching on the person of Jesus and his death and Resurrection. I have tried to do the same. Before dealing with the sacraments I have inserted a further chapter on prayer, having touched on it previously in the 'Enquiry Stage'. Prayer is, after all, the very basis of our Christian life of faith. The fruit of prayer and the sacraments should be seen in our behaviour. Hence, following the sacraments is the section on 'Love in Action'.

Father Anthony de Mello, SJ, once said that the shortest distance between the human mind and truth is by the story. It is for this reason that I have tried to punctuate the presentation with some appropriate stories, and I am deeply indebted to Tony de Mello, both for his inspiration and help in prayer, as well as for some of the stories which come from his books.

Many people who start to come to Mass either before or during the enquiry stage need to have some basic knowledge of the structure of this principal act of worship. This is, therefore, included in the preliminary stages, but developed, giving something of its Jewish and pagan background in the main instructional session, and then touched on again in the Lenten period.

Each topic concludes with four practical suggestions:

- Prayer for the beginning or end of each session *and* to be used at home during the ensuing week.
- Topics for discussion in a group or in pairs.
- Scripture readings, also to be pondered on during the week.
- Books that may be bought or borrowed by those wishing to read more deeply on a particular subject.

Inevitably many topics have been omitted, but one of the tasks of the sponsor, the Catholic who journeys with the enquirer, is to fill in some of the gaps, and to share a little of that peculiar Catholic culture which is 'caught rather than taught'. A few of the chapters include material that will certainly require further explanation, preferably by the catechist, leader of the group or priest. Some topics, by their nature and importance, have given rise to longer sections, which means more to be covered that particular week.

On the other hand, and depending on the number of weeks available for the sessions, chapters eight, eleven, twenty-one and some others may quite easily be divided. Some may also prefer to combine the APPETISER sessions with the MAIN COURSE, and then, in the early stages, give more time for sharing and listening to one another's 'faith stories'.

It really *is* important to have someone alongside you, to help you, to offer a hand when needed. I heard once of a commercial traveller who, whenever he arrived at a town on a Saturday night, would invite someone or other he might meet, at the hotel, or in the course of his work, to accompany him to Mass on the Sunday morning...

I myself, in my teens, as a non-Catholic, used to visit an elderly French lady who helped me with the language. At the end of one of the French lessons I found myself asking if I might accompany her to Mass the following Sunday. She was surprised, pleased and welcoming... and it was thanks to this that I later came into the Church and subsequently became a priest.

Finally, the title of the book came to me as I was putting some finishing touches to it on the feast of St Thomas the Apostle. Thomas was devastated by Jesus's Crucifixion and, in his grief, kept away from the rest of the group and wasn't there when Jesus showed himself to them. When he heard the others recounting the appearance of the Risen Lord, he refused to believe. Then Jesus appeared again when Thomas was there.

'Stretch out your hand,' Jesus said to him, showing the wounds of the Crucifixion.

Thomas found faith. 'My Lord and my God,' he exclaimed, with total faith and love and trust.

Jesus then said to him, 'You have believed because you have seen me. Blessed are those who have not seen and who have believed.'

My prayer for you who read this book is that it may help you who have not seen, to believe.

Ken Payne
Feast of St Thomas, Apostle,
3rd July 1997

Contents

Introduction xi

THE APPETISER: General Introductory Sessions

1. Who Are We and What Is It All About? 19
2. A Look Around the Church 27
3. Faith and Prayer 32
4. Introduction to the Mass 40

THE MAIN COURSE: Instruction

5. Existence of God...? Existence of Jesus...? 47
6. Jesus's Background: The Old Testament 60
7. The Witness of the Early Christians: The New Testament 68
8. Jesus: His Life and Death 74
9. Jesus: His Resurrection and the Trinity 82
10. The Church Founded by Jesus: The People of God 93
11. The Church: Its Authority and Organisation; Mary, its First Member 102
12. The Basis of Our Life of Faith: Prayer 110
13. The Sacraments in General: Signs of God's Love 122

14. The Sacraments of Baptism and Confirmation 129
15. The Sacrament of Holy Orders 138
16. The Sacrament of Marriage 145
17. The Sacrament of Reconciliation 156
18. The Sacrament of the Sick 166
19. The Background to the Eucharist: The Passover 176
20. The Eucharist: The Real Presence 185
21. Love in Action: Christian Morality 195
22. Rebirth: Death and After 211
23. The Church through the Centuries 220
24. The Church Today: Ecumenism 226

THE DESSERT: Lenten Period

25. Lent: Reflecting on the Past and Looking Forward to Easter (First Week of Lent) 237
26. Faith in and Devotion to the Bread of Life (Second Week of Lent) 240
27. Confession (Third Week of Lent) 247
28. Coming In (Fourth Week of Lent) 253
29. Retreat (Fifth Week of Lent) 258
30. The Easter Vigil (Sixth Week of Lent) 259

THE COFFEE: Eastertide

31. Preparing for Pentecost and After 263

Conclusion 268

THE APPETISER

General Introductory Sessions

Chapter One

Who Are We and What Is It All About?

In a Group

Most people feel quite strange and rather shy at first as they come together. You may well find yourself in quite a mixed group of people, but hopefully you will be with a practising Catholic whom you know and this will give you confidence! The group may number anything from two or three up to thirty or forty people, and sometimes more.

There may not only be some practising Catholics, but a mix of practising Christians from other Churches, those not baptised in any denomination, Catholics who want a 'wash and brush-up' on their faith and so on. The first session usually begins with each person introducing themselves, giving their name and saying something about themselves and their religious background.

Welcome

The most important aspect of this initial session is to make the newcomer feel welcome. Prospective sponsors and other members of the parish should be present. They should not be there as representatives of groups or organisations, but as individuals who are willing to share their faith, to say what makes them tick; people who are able to share something of the struggles and bereavements, the crosses as well as the joys and high moments they have experienced in their attempts to follow the way of Jesus Christ.

Shortly before I became a Catholic myself, I recall staying with a family and, through them, really getting 'the smell' of Catholicism from their attitude to worldly goods, their practice of prayer and a complete sense of trust in the providence of God.

One essential part of these preliminary weeks or months is, therefore, to link the enquirer to people in the parish who will welcome one or two into their homes for a cup of coffee. These need not be families. It could be an elderly person living alone who would be glad of a visit, and willing to talk about their faith and how they pray. The personal story, simply and honestly recounted, can have a great impact. Many in the parish can become involved in this way, as it is thus that many things we take for granted in our faith can be explained to the enquirer.

However, it is not just one-way traffic! The newcomer also has something to give. We can all learn from one another, and someone from another Church must not feel they have to start all over again and betray their roots.

There is no one way to approach this initial APPETISER stage. Each group of enquirers will be different. Each parish welcoming them will have different resources. Indeed, each year the approach will vary; but the essential constituent is the welcome and hospitality shown, not in an overpowering and dogmatic way, but with gentleness and respect for the other's freedom and background. Whereas each person has a slightly different journey to make, it is all the time the same Lord beckoning to us and calling for a conversion of mind, heart and lifestyle.

The welcome, then, is more than a pleasant smile, a few words or a handshake. It is a real effort towards hospitality, regardless of whether we have much to share or very little. It is a real ministry and just as important as the talks which take place during the MAIN COURSE of the meal which follows.

It is during this initial period that the key human-life questions should rear their heads, such as:

- Is there any purpose to life?
- Why is there evil in the world if God is good?
- Is it possible to have unity and peace among humans?
- Why is life so often unfair?

There will also be more personal questions, along the lines of:

- If I go to Mass, how will I know when to stand up and sit down?
- Why do Catholics confess to a priest?

- Why don't Catholics sing more, and better?

It is important to give at least a brief answer to such questions at this stage, but there should also be the assurance that they will be dealt with more fully at a later date.

It follows then, from what has been said, that this early part of 'the meal' should extend over a period of time, being interspersed with a number of visits and contact with parishioners exercising their ministry of hospitality and welcome.

You Are Special

Remember that each person is different. *You* are very special, and subsequent to your sharing individually with a friend or when visiting a member of the parish, you may wish to share with the whole group.

> In all the world there is nobody, nobody like you. Since the beginning of time there has never been another person like you. Nobody has your smile, your eyes, your hands, your hair. Nobody owns your handwriting, your voice. You are special.
>
> Nobody can paint your brush-strokes. Nobody has your taste for food, or music, or dance or art. Nobody in the universe sees things as you do. In all time there has never been anyone who laughs in exactly your way; and what makes you laugh, or cry, or think, may provoke a totally different response in another. So... you are special.
>
> You are different from any other person who has ever lived in the history of the universe. You are the only one in the whole creation who has your particular set of abilities. There is always someone who is

> better at one thing or another. Every person is my superior in at least one way. Nobody in the universe can reach the quality of the combination of your talents, your feelings. Like a roomful of musical instruments, some might excel in one way or another, but nobody can match the symphonic sound produced when all are played together. Your symphony.
>
> Through all eternity no one will ever walk, talk, think or do exactly as you. You are special. You are rare and in all rarity there is enormous value, and because of your great value the need for you to imitate anyone else is absolutely wrong. You are special and it is no accident that you are so.
>
> Please realise that God made you for a special purpose. He has a job for you to do that nobody else can do as well as you can. Out of a billion applicants only one is qualified. Only one has the unique and right combination of what it takes, and that one is you. You are special.

So, *your* personal story is going to be helpful to others in the group, as well as enabling you to appreciate better how God has been working in your life.

Purpose of the Sessions

The whole programme is designed to give you information about the Catholic faith, but more importantly, its purpose is to help you grow in love and faith. Faith is a gift, and if in a few months you find yourself saying, 'Well, that's fine, thank you very much. I understand more about the Catholic Church, but I don't think I want to do any more about it at the moment,' you are completely free, and there will be no pressure whatsoever put on you to go any further.

It is a 'journey in faith', and most will find that they will grow in faith and love through the talks, discussions and sharing, but most of all through prayer, both during the session and also each day at home. If you go to the sessions with a partner or a friend who is a practising Catholic, this person will perhaps be your 'companion on the journey', and if you eventually decide that it is God's will that you are received into the Church, he or she will then be your sponsor (or godparent if you are not baptised).

The PEANUTS cartoon at the beginning of this section expresses the importance of 'being in the right room' – of following the will of God. Yes, we do want to know the secret of life: what is man and the meaning of his life? What are we here for? We believe that the answer to these questions is to be found in its fullness through faith in Jesus Christ. All that this involves will be spelt out gradually in subsequent sessions.

We have a great destiny. Take a moment or two to ponder the following de Mello story.

A man found an eagle's egg and put it in the nest of a backyard hen. The eaglet hatched with the brood of chicks and grew up with them. All his life the eagle did what the backyard chickens did, thinking he was a backyard chicken. He scratched the earth for worms and insects. He clucked and cackled. And he would thrash his wings and fly a few feet into the air like the chicken. After all, that is how a chicken is supposed to fly, isn't it?

Years passed and the eagle grew very old. One day he saw a magnificent bird far above him in the cloudless sky. It floated in graceful majesty among the powerful wind currents, with scarcely a beat of its strong golden wings.

The old eagle looked up in awe. 'Who's that?' he said to his neighbour.

'That's the eagle, the king of the birds,' said his neighbour. 'But don't give it another thought. You and I are different from him.'

So the eagle never gave it another thought. He died thinking he was a backyard chicken.

Prayer for this Session and During the Week

In a few minutes of silence, thank God for any one person with you in your group. Tell God how grateful you are to various people who have come into your past life and helped you. When on your own, spend as long as you wish doing this.

End by saying slowly and with care:

Our Father,
who art in heaven,
hallowed be thy name.
Thy kingdom come,
thy will be done on earth, as it is in heaven.
Give us this day our daily bread,
and forgive us our trespasses,
as we forgive those who trespass against us,
and lead us not into temptation,
but deliver us from evil. Amen.

? *For Discussion*

What three things do you want to know about the Catholic Church?

Scripture Reading

Acts 22:1–16

For Further Reading

The Christian Response by Michel Quoist
Awareness by Anthony de Mello (Fount Paperbacks)

Chapter Two
A Look Around the Church

A visit to a church with a *brief* explanation of what is seen there is useful at this stage. A full account of the meaning behind and the reason for many of the things seen and experienced in a Catholic church will be left to a later occasion – so at this stage you must be patient!

Holy Water

As you enter you will notice a small receptacle containing water. This is a holy water stoup. It contains blessed water (anything that is blessed is set aside for a holy purpose), and it is the custom on going into church to dip one's fingers in the water and make the sign of the cross, saying, 'In the name of the Father, and of the Son, and of the Holy Spirit,' as a reminder that we are baptised into the death and Resurrection of Christ. We make use of many 'things' and signs to help us focus on the spiritual. It is rather like two people who love each other: they need to show that love by outward signs...

Way of the Cross

Around the walls of the church you will usually find representations of some of the stages leading up to Jesus's Crucifixion and Resurrection. They are known as the Stations of the Cross. Years ago there were sometimes up to forty of them. Now they are mostly reduced to fourteen or fifteen and are the focus for meditation on the sufferings of Jesus, which is a particular devotion during the weeks leading up to Easter, the celebration of his death and Resurrection.

Other pictures and statues may remind us of the patron saint of the church, and there is always, of course, one of Our Lady, Mary, the greatest of the saints. Again, these serve as reminders for us. Just as a person may have a photo of their deceased parents on the mantelpiece, so we have pictures and statues of the saints, those we believe led good lives and are with God in heaven.

Lectern, Altar and Chair

Now we come to the main part of the church – the sanctuary area. For the public worship of the Catholic Church, three focal points are used: the lectern, from which the scriptures are read; the altar, where the bread and wine are offered and become the Real Presence of Jesus Christ; and the celebrant's chair, from which the priest presides over the worship.

Tabernacle

Some of the consecrated bread (called the 'Host') is kept in a 'tabernacle', so that it may be taken at any time to the sick or dying. Wherever the tabernacle is kept also serves as an important place for private prayer and adoration. In some churches the tabernacle, identified by a veil and/or a small light, is situated near the altar, whilst in others it is in a separate chapel suitable for devotional prayer.

Most Catholics genuflect, that is, go down on one knee, when they pass in front of the tabernacle containing the Blessed Sacrament. This is a sign of reverence and of faith.

It is also good to spend a few minutes in prayer there whilst in church.

Font and Confessional

Two other important areas in the church are the font, where baptisms take place and Christians begin their journey in and with Christ, and the confessional, where the renewal of baptismal strength and forgiveness occurs.

Candles

You will probably notice candles burning, perhaps in front of a statue. These are homely reminders of someone who has prayed there and who has made this small outward sign of their prayer continuing, even after they have left. They express our love of God and his love of us – a love relationship that burns on and dispels the darkness. Candles are also used by the Church at Mass, at the Easter Vigil service and at baptisms. Light is important for all living things. Light also enables us to see where we are going. Christ is the Light of the World, enabling us to see where we are going in our lives. Hence the symbolism of candles at the Easter Vigil and at baptism – the Easter candle, symbol of the Resurrected Christ. But why candles at Mass? The reason lies in the fact that lamps were lit at the paschal meal. The Last Supper was a paschal meal, and so we light candles which have a new meaning because Christ, the Light of the World, becomes present on the altar. Lamps and candles were also very necessary when Mass was celebrated in the catacombs underground in Rome, when the early Christians were being persecuted.

Incense

You may sometimes notice a smell of incense. This is a very ancient sign of reverence and prayer. It also has the useful function of purifying the air after a church has been full of people for an hour or so!

You may also see people sitting (not necessarily just having a rest – it expresses and helps receptive and contemplative attention); kneeling (which expresses and can facilitate private prayer, penance, humility and adoration); and standing (which expresses vigilance, thanksgiving and respect, and reminds us that we are called to be resurrected beings).

Finally, as you walk around and look, think not only of the past and our whole Catholic tradition going back to Jesus Christ himself, but also of the present faithful users who come each weekend, using it as their regular place of worship, those who use it frequently in the week as a place for silent prayer, and all who pray and work together to try to make it a living and loving community of followers of the Lord.

✠ *Prayers for this Session and During the Week*

Father,
pour out your Spirit upon your people,
  and grant us,
  a new vision of your glory
  a new experience of your power
  a new faithfulness to your Word

and a new consecration to your service,
so that your love may grow among us.
Show us the way ahead,
so that your kingdom may come,
through Christ Our Lord
Amen.

A MOTORIST'S PRAYER

Give me a steady hand, a watchful eye,
That none may suffer hurt when I pass by.
Thou givest life; I pray no act of mine
May take away or mar that gift of Thine.
Shield those, dear Lord, who bear me company,
From foolish folk and all calamity.
Teach me to use my car for others' need.
Let me not miss, through witless love of speed,
The beauties of thy world. That thus I may
With joy and courtesy go on my way.

(Authorship and copyright unknown)

? *For Discussion*

What did you see in the church that particularly interested you?

Scripture Reading

Acts 20:7–12

For Further Reading

A guidebook or history of your local parish church, if available.

Chapter Three
Faith and Prayer

We believe many things on the testimony of other people. We are called to believe in 'things unseen' on the testimony of people down the ages. However, faith is a gift, and Christian faith, first and foremost, is faith in a person – that of God himself and the revelation he made of himself in Jesus Christ. Knowledge of what this involves is important and helps, but because faith is a gift from God it comes primarily through the opening of ourselves to God in prayer.

Fear

The reverse of faith is fear, and the most frequent injunction found on Jesus's lips is the phrase, 'Do not be afraid...' Fear really means that we are centred on ourselves rather than 'another'. It is a failure to trust. My parents always had an inscription hanging in their bedroom: 'Fear knocked at the door. Faith opened it. And there was no one there.' In the following story of the two frogs it was fear that caused the first frog to drown.

Two frogs fell into a tub full of cream and since neither of them had learnt to swim it looked as though they would die. One of the frogs was the kind who always looked upon the black side of things. He was what is called a 'pessimist'. He lost heart and said, 'I'm finished. I can't do anything about it. I will never get out of this mess,' and he sank to the bottom and was drowned. The second frog was frightened, but he was the kind of frog who always looked on the bright side of things – the kind we call an 'optimist'. He refused to give in easily. 'I'm not going to die,' he cried. And he began to do his best to try and swim. He kept on trying, thrashing with his legs. Suddenly, to his immense surprise, he found himself on the top of a great lump of butter. His struggles had turned the cream into butter and so he was able to hop out.

Faith and Trust

Faith, then, is not merely holding on to a purely intellectual statement of belief, like the Creed, carrying it around like a handbag; nor is it just a question of the emotions, saying, 'I feel that such-and-such is true'; nor must it be confused with magic and superstition, like the person who thinks he has to say a certain prayer X times in order to guarantee a particular result. No. Faith engages the whole person – intellect, will and emotions – and it means believing in the sense of accepting, being involved with, being committed to and, above all, trusting God and Jesus Christ whom he has sent.

This trust is to be found in many of the people we read about in the Bible and in the history of the Church. Abraham let God direct his life and so did Moses, the Apostles, St Margaret of Cortona, St Ignatius and countless others: all were ordinary people who placed their lives in God's hands. Faith, then, means to entrust oneself to God. The Hebrew word 'Amen' is our response to this gift from God, and for us it means, 'Yes, I believe you, Lord.'

A few years ago a terrorist bomb exploded in Enniskillen. Gordon Wilson and his twenty year old daughter, Marie, were buried in the rubble. During the appalling ordeal while they waited to be rescued, Gordon called out to his daughter just near him:

'Are you all right, dear?'

'Yes,' she replied.

Again he called out, and again she replied, five times in all.

The fifth time she added, 'Daddy, I love you,' and then said no more.

She had died and Gordon, after he was rescued, said, 'I bear no ill will: that sort of talk is not going to bring her back to life. Don't ask me for a purpose. I don't have a purpose, an answer. But I know there has to be a plan. It's part of a greater plan, and God is good, and we shall meet again.'

That is faith. It is a gift, and Jesus himself, confronted with one of the Apostles who did not find faith easy, said, 'Blessed are those who have not seen and yet believe.' (John 20:29)

Prayer

The primary expression of our faith is in prayer. This is why it is a good idea to begin each of the sessions with five to ten minutes of prayer, and in so doing introduce some of the many different ways of praying practised by Christians. Hopefully, this will be an encouragement to spend time in prayer on your own each day – laying yourself open trustfully for the power and guidance of God to permeate your whole being.

Our relationship with God is a relationship of love, and as with the love between two people, we have to give it time. This is the first and most important thing to remember about prayer-time. The place of prayer and our bodily attitude are also important. It is true that we can pray anywhere, but obviously some places are better than others. At this stage I am thinking of private, personal prayer, and even for this an empty church is often found to be the best place; perhaps others like to be out in the country; while some choose a particular corner of a room at home. Visual aids, such as a crucifix or statue, can also be useful – though not essential.

People often think they have to kneel down to pray. This is not so, and indeed is often not the best attitude for concentration. An upright chair (*not* an armchair) in which you can sit with your back straight is a good attentive position. Lying on your back on the floor is also good, but best of all, for some at least, is the prayer stool. In all these the back is kept straight, and this seems to be important.

Prayer and Silence

The problem many people have with prayer is concentration, and being able to bring their thoughts into the present. A good means of doing this is to be aware of the following:

- The sensations in your body, from the top of your head, face, neck and chest, right down to the feel of your feet on the floor. Do this a number of times.
- The sounds around you – in the room and from outside. Do not wish they were not there; just accept them as sounds of God's world.
- Your breathing. No need to breathe deeply or differently, but just be aware of the air going in through your nostrils, into your lungs and out again.

These, and other similar exercises, are really the beginnings of prayer, and enable us to realise that the all-important time for us is the present moment. The more we come to live in the present, as opposed to the past (common to many people as they become older), the more we shall find true peace and joy.

Having prepared ourselves in this way, we can remain in silence, use some set prayers, take a passage from Scripture and consider it, talk to God in our own words, or pray in any one of the many different ways we shall be using in the course of the instructional sessions later on. In all prayer, praise and gratitude are most important. Unfortunately, when we think of prayer, we so often think of asking God for this or that. Such prayer of petition, or intercessory prayer, is important, but it is by no means the whole story! Perhaps the following de Mello story will make the point.

The Lord Vishnu was so tired of his devotee's constant petitions that he appeared to him one day and said: 'I have decided to grant you any three things you ask for. After that, I shall give you nothing more.'

The devotee delightedly made his first petition at once. He asked that his wife should die so that he could marry a better woman. His petition was immediately granted. But when friends and relatives gathered for the funeral and began to recall all the good qualities of his wife, the devotee realised he had been hasty. He now realised he had been quite blind to all her virtues. Was he likely to find another woman quite as good as her? So he asked the Lord to bring her back to life!

That left him with just one petition. And he was determined not to make a mistake this time, for he would have no chance to correct it.

He consulted widely. Some of his friends advised him to ask for immortality. But of what good was immortality, said others, if he did not have good health? And of what use was health if he had no money? And of what use was money if he had no friends?

Years passed and he could not make up his mind what to ask for: life or health or wealth or power or love. Finally he said to the Lord, 'Please advise me on what to ask for.'

The Lord laughed when he saw the man's predicament, and said, 'Ask to be contented no matter what life brings you.'

The Still Point

Probably man's most fantastic invention of all time was the wheel. And, apart from the wheel being the basic means of movement and the basis of all machinery, there is something else quite extraordinary about it.

Just think for a moment of a large cartwheel. There's the hub and the spokes and the rim... And if you were a little fly settled on the rim while the wheel was going round, you would be forever moving, you would become giddy. However, if you crawled down one of the spokes, the nearer you got to the centre, the less you would move, and right at the centre, *there is a point that is quite still.*

Now, I think we are rather like the fly on the wheel: we are so often on the rim, far from the centre, and our lives seem to be in turmoil... *God is at the still point, at the centre. And to find God there is the basis of peace,* and comes about through time spent in prayer.

Our Faith Journey

Frances Parkinson Keyes quotes the following in the account of her conversion to Catholicism (*The Road to Damascus* Vol. 1, 1949).

I must go forth upon a pilgrim's journey;
Along a strange and dimly hidden road;
I cannot see what joy or care is waiting for me there,
nor can I tell its length or test my load.
But this I know:
That faith will light my journey,
and mercy share the burden I must bring;
That love divine will ever tread the road with me,
and lead the pilgrim to the palace of the King.

The road I'll take upon my pilgrim's journey,
may tread its way through sunny valleys fair;
May be in gloom, may even lead where danger waits for me,
and I may find both joy and sorrow there.
But this I know:
That faith will light my journey,
and mercy share the burden I must bring;
That love divine will ever tread the road with me,
and lead the pilgrim to the palace of the King.

✣ *Prayers for this Session and During the Week*

Let nothing disturb you,
let nothing frighten you,
though all things pass,
God does not change.
Patience wins all things
but he lacks nothing
who possesses God,
for God alone suffices.
(St Teresa of Avila)

God be in my head
and in my understanding.
God be in mine eyes
and in my looking.
God be in my mouth
and in my speaking.
God be in my heart
and in my thinking.

God be at mine end
and at my departing.
(Sarum Primer, 1527)

GLORY BE TO THE FATHER

Glory be to the Father, and to the Son, and to the Holy Spirit.
As it was in the beginning, is now, and ever shall be,
world without end.
Amen.

? For Discussion

Who is the happiest person you know?
What do you think is the secret of their happiness?

Scripture Reading

Psalm 27
Matthew 10:26–31

For Further Reading

Pray all Ways by Edward Hays (Forest of Peace Books, USA)
The Christian Response by Michel Quoist
Awareness by Anthony de Mello

Chapter Four
Introduction to the Mass

There are many different forms of worship in the Church. In the last session we saw something of the diversity of private, personal prayer. This can open out into prayer with a few others, with a group or with a larger gathering of people. Morning and Evening Prayer, which follow a set structure (psalms, Scripture reading, prayers of intercession and so on) are used in religious communities, by all priests and many lay people. There are further forms of prayer for different times of day and different occasions, for use individually or with a number of people gathered together.

Going to Mass

The most important act of worship for all is the Mass, which Catholics take part in celebrating every Sunday (or Saturday evening, as following Jewish custom the holy day begins the night before), and certain other special feast days. If you have not already begun participating in the Mass, it would be important at this stage to begin, even though you may still be puzzled by all sorts of things you experience when you are there! It is rather like learning to swim. It is no good standing on the edge of the pool: you have to get in, splash around and make lots of mistakes before you finally master the strokes. So get in the water! Go to Mass on Sunday, preferably with your sponsor or someone who can guide you a little.

The Structure of the Mass

What follows now is a very brief guide to the structure of the Mass to help you through these initial steps. We will be looking at the whole background to the Mass and the reasons for worshipping God in this way much later on. This is, after all, just an appetiser!

THE FIRST PART

After the priest has welcomed everyone and introduced the Mass, we are either reminded again of our Baptism, so important is this, or we reflect in sorrow for a moment on our sins and failings. On most Sundays a hymn of praise is said or sung (the Gloria is one of the oldest Christian hymns), and the priest brings together our individual prayers with a prayer called the Collect. We then sit for the readings (from the Old Testament and/or the New Testament, showing something of God's love and care for his people), but stand for the reading of the Gospel – out of respect especially for the words of Jesus, the Son of God. This is followed by the homily, when the priest will usually expand or explain some aspect of what we have just heard. The silence following this is to allow us to ponder and digest this first part of the Mass.

THE SECOND PART

The creed, or the profession of faith, and the prayers of intercession form a kind of interlude, albeit a significant part of the Mass, before we move into the second part. Here the gifts of bread and wine are brought to the altar, a collection is taken, the Church being dependent on this for the costs of its general running, upkeep, schools, clergy and suchlike. The priest then proclaims the central prayer of the Mass, the Eucharistic Prayer, during which the gifts of bread and wine are changed into the Real Presence of Jesus Christ.

Shortly after everyone has prayed together the Lord's Prayer, the Our Father, it is usual in most churches to exchange a sign of peace. This is an opportunity to express our love and concern for those around us before sharing the one bread which is Jesus Christ.

Catholics then receive their Lord in Holy Communion. This may be 'under both kinds' of bread and wine, now changed into Christ Himself, or it may be under just 'one kind'. Similarly, in many churches, non-Catholics, and Catholics who for some reason cannot receive Communion, are invited to go forward with the others and ask for a blessing from the priest or deacon, or a prayer from the special minister distributing Holy Communion. Trained lay people help the priest in this, as well as taking part in the readings earlier in the Mass.

THE DISMISSAL

The Mass ends with the concluding prayer, blessing and dismissal. It is from what used to be the last words of the Mass in Latin, *Ite missa est*, that the name 'Mass' derived. The Latin phrase means, 'Go, you are sent', and that is just what we are: sent to put into practice what we have heard and experienced.

The basic structure of the Mass is always the same – although in some parts of the world there are variations, different rites, as they are termed. However, the readings and some of the prayers vary from day to day, and the celebration may change in style according to which parts are sung, and how the music is arranged. (For the Rite of Acceptance as a catechumen see p.40 of the Rite.)

✝ *Prayers for this Session and During the Week*

Glory to God in the highest
and peace to His people on earth.
Lord God, heavenly King, Almighty God and Father,
We worship you, we give you thanks,
we praise you for your glory.
Lord Jesus Christ, only Son of the Father,
Lord God, lamb of God;
you take away the sin of the world;
have mercy on us;
you are seated at the right hand of the Father:
receive our prayer.
For you alone are the Holy One,
you alone are the Lord:
You alone are the Most High, Jesus Christ,
with the Holy Spirit in the glory of God the Father. Amen.

(From the Mass)

? *For Discussion*

When you have been to Mass, what is it you have found most difficult to follow?

Scripture Reading

Matthew 26:26–29

For Further Reading

What it Means Being Married to a Catholic (Redemptorist Publications)

The Simple Prayer Book (CTS)

(This would, in fact, be good to purchase; it is very cheap and includes the main prayers of the Mass and other Catholic devotions.)

THE MAIN COURSE
Instruction

Chapter Five
Existence of God...? Existence of Jesus...?

There may be some of you who question the existence of God, or who, at times, perhaps when great suffering has hit you, have just wondered... And then, going on a step further, you may have had doubts about this person, Jesus Christ – did he really exist? What evidence do we have? So in this first session of our MAIN COURSE of the meal, we will address ourselves to those two questions.

Denial of God

The problem of God is the most important of all. It is the most basic. The German philosopher, Nietzsche, triumphantly proclaimed: 'God is dead!' This is the attitude of some today, but it takes on different forms.

- There is a sort of practical atheism of those who do not actually deny God, but who live as if he did not exist. They believe only what they see and don't wish to complicate life by posing questions. Religion, in any form, is a matter of taste, like sport or music or politics.
- There are also those for whom the notion of God was useful in the past as an explanation of things more recently explained and understood by modern science

and technology. Science has made the 'God hypothesis' out of date.

- Karl Marx, and others, maintained that there is only 'matter' and 'activity'. It is through activity and work that the universe evolves and man progresses. Art, poetry, morality and so on, are merely 'superstructures', relics of an age of ignorance. God is a sort of scarecrow which the rich used in order to enslave the poor. Religion is an opium and atheism must one day emancipate and liberate man by means of science and work.
- Sartre, the French philosopher, proclaimed that God is impossible. Since I exist and I am free, then the existence of a god would deny my liberty. I cannot be a creature and free at the same time. I am free, therefore I am not created. Therefore, I create myself; and so God does not exist!
- Then there are those who have what one might describe as a humanistic idea of God, which often amounts to a disbelief in the god we are speaking of. They are the ones who think of God as 'an old man up there', or a glorified telephone operator plugging into people's prayers, or a judge/policeman type of figure, or even a high-powered hospital administrator!

However, to deny God doesn't stop him existing, any more than drawing the curtains on a sunny day prevents the sun from being there. To fight against God does not mean to say that one hasn't a hunger and thirst for him. Dostoyevsky, in *The Possessed*, makes this remark:

> The perfect atheism is right at the top of the ladder, on the last rung which leads to perfect faith.

Some are atheist through a thirst for the Absolute, and because they cannot be content with the god that is presented to them – often a god who is unjust or cruel or indifferent or nationalistic. Man does seek the One True God, whether he realises it or not. Denial of God is, paradoxically, a seeking of him.

Pointers to God

So much for the negation of God. What of the 'pointers' to the existence of God? The intricate workings of the engine and equipment of a jet airliner point immediately to a designer's mind and plan. Similarly, when we consider the complexity and order built into the very nature of the macrocosm (the very large: the vastness of the universe and so on) and the microcosm (the very small: the laws governing atoms, electrons, protons and so on), then it is surely difficult to deny the existence of a supreme mind behind it all. Einstein, one of the world's greatest scientists, realised this.

Then there are our everyday experiences of the wonder and beauty of nature, of a sunset or of stillness and silence (though perhaps more difficult to experience these days). Mystical experiences may also point to a 'beyond'. However, we must tread carefully here, as they are not for everyone; and there are many laws of nature, not yet understood, that may well be found, one day, to embrace some so-called mystical phenomena.

Perhaps the great preacher, Bossuet, summed it all up in this simple and clear statement:

> If there had been a single instant when nothing existed, nothing would exist to all eternity. Therefore, since something does exist, from all eternity *Being* has existed.

You need to ponder that for a moment! If there had been a single instant when nothing existed, nothing would exist to all eternity. But, since there are beings, since we *do* exist, this means that Being is eternal. God is hence a reality without limit, infinite, complete, absolute, unique. And if he is completeness and infinity, then he is LOVE... *and it is in and through love that we find the most important pointer of all to God*.

The universe is not, then, the product of blindly determined material forces. It is the result of an infinite mind, God, who is both transcendent ('beyond' and 'outside' his creation) and, at the same time, imminent (present through his nature which is love, in the very heart and depth of every part of that creation). It is appropriate to recall the story of the elephant who was enjoying a leisurely dip in a jungle pool. A rat came up to the pool and insisted that the elephant got out.

'I won't,' said the elephant. 'I'm enjoying myself and I refuse to be disturbed.'

'I insist you get out this minute,' said the rat.

'Why?' said the elephant.

'I shall tell you only after you are out of the pool,' said the rat.

'Then I won't get out,' said the elephant. But he eventually gave in. He lumbered out of the pool, stood in front of the rat and said, 'Now then, why did you want me to get out of the pool?'

'To check if you were wearing my swimming trunks,' said the rat!

It is infinitely easier for an elephant to get into the trunks of a rat than for God to fit into our notions of him. Or, as Tolstoy has it:

> If the thought comes to you that everything that you have thought about God is mistaken and that there is

> no God, do not be dismayed. It happens to many people. But do not think that the source of our unbelief is that there is no God. If you no longer believe in the God in whom you believed before, this comes from the fact that there was something wrong with your belief, and you must strive to grasp better that which you call God. When a savage ceases to believe in his wooden God, this does not mean that there is no God, but only that the true God is not of wood.

We shall see later how the nature of this God is spelt out and revealed to us in Jesus Christ through his Church; but for the moment, let us look briefly at the evidence for the existence of this man, Jesus, who lived in Palestine two thousand years ago.

Non-Catholic Sources: References to Jesus

Several of these mention him and the existence of his followers.

- In AD 64, on the occasion of the Great Fire of Rome, the Emperor Nero tried to avoid blame by accusing Christians of causing it. 'Nero put in his own place culprits and punished with every refinement of cruelty the men whom the common people hated for their secret crimes. They called them Christians. Christ, from whom the name was given, had been put to death in the reign of Tiberius by the procurator Pontius Pilate, and the persistent superstition checked for a while.' (Tacitus, who was proconsul of Asia, wrote this in his *Annals* at the beginning of the second century.)

- Tranquillus was for a time secretary to the Emperor Hadrian, and in AD 121 he wrote concerning Nero,

'Punishment was inflicted on the Christians, a class of men addicted to a novel and mischievous superstition.'

- Only fragments remain of the writings of Thallus, dated about AD 52. However, Julius Africanus, a Christian, later refers to his account of the Crucifixion:

  As to his works severally, and his cures effected upon body and soul, and the mysteries of his doctrine, and the resurrection from the dead, these have been most authoritatively set forth by his disciples and apostles before us. On the whole world there pressed a most fearful darkness; and the rocks were rent by an earthquake, and many places in Judea and other districts were thrown down. This darkness Thallus, in the third book of his *History*, calls, as appears to me without reason, an eclipse of the sun. For the Hebrews celebrate the Passover on the fourteenth day according to the moon, and the passion of our Saviour falls on the day before the Passover; but an eclipse of the sun takes place only when the moon comes under the sun. And it cannot happen at any other time but in the interval between the first day of the new moon and the last day of the old, that is, at their junction: how then should an eclipse be supposed to happen when the moon is almost diametrically opposite the sun? Let that opinion pass however; let it carry the majority with it; and let this portent of the world be deemed an eclipse of the sun, like others portent only to the eye. Phlegon records that, in the time of Tiberius Caesar, at full moon, there was a full eclipse of the sun from the sixth hour to the ninth – manifestly that one of which we speak. But what has an eclipse in common with an earthquake, the rending rocks, and the resurrection of the dead, and so great a perturbation throughout the universe? Surely no such event as this is recorded for a long period. But it was a darkness induced by God, because the Lord happened then to suffer. And calculation makes out that the period of seventy weeks, as noted in Daniel, is completed at this time.

- Around AD 112, Pliny the Younger, who was for a time governor of Bithynia, wrote as follows in a letter to the Emperor Trajan:

  ...this is the course I have taken with those who were accused before me as Christians. I asked at their own lips whether they were Christians, and if they confessed, I asked them a second and third time with threats of punishment. If they kept to it, I ordered them for execution... Others who were named by the informer said that they were Christians and then denied it, explaining that they had been, but had ceased to be such, some three years ago, some a good many years, and a few as many as twenty. All these too not only worshipped your statue and the images of the gods, but cursed Christ. They maintained, however, that the amount of their fault or error had been this, that it was their habit on a fixed day to assemble before daylight and sing by turns a hymn to Christ as a god; and that they bound themselves with an oath, not for any crime, but not to commit theft or robbery or adultery, not to break their word, and not to deny a deposit when demanded.

- Flavius Josephus, born in AD 37, was a Jewish Pharisee, and led the Jewish resistance in Galilee about AD 70. On capture and being brought to Vespasian, he was liberated as he prophesied that Vespasian would become Emperor. He later wrote a propaganda book on the history of the Jews, designed to deter his fellow Jews from revolting against Rome. The following extract is from his book, *Antiquities* 18.3:

> Now, there was about this time, Jesus, wise man, if it be lawful to call him a man, for he was a doer of wonderful works – a teacher of such men as receive the truth with pleasure. He drew over to him both many of the Jews and many of the Gentiles. He was [the] Christ and when Pilate, at the suggestion of the principal men amongst us, had condemned him to the cross, those that loved him at the first did not forsake him, for he appeared to them alive again the third day, as the divine prophets had foretold these and ten thousand other wonderful things concerning him; and the tribe of Christians, so named from him, are not extinct at this day.

These are just some of the references to Jesus and his followers in the early years. In addition to these, Christian documents, of course, abound, and most of what we know about Jesus is derived from them.

Archaeology

Archaeology has revealed two highly significant indications of the spread of the Christian faith. The Roman town of Herculaneum was destroyed in AD 79 by the eruption of Vesuvius. In the upper part of a house a large cross was discovered on the wall. There is no known pagan explanation for this. Also found there was a Christian acrostic word square. These were fairly common later on, but this is the earliest known example.

R	O	T	A	S
O	P	E	R	A
T	E	N	E	T
A	R	E	P	O
S	A	T	O	R

Translated: 'AREPO THE SOWER GRASPS [OR HOLDS] THE WHEELS'.

The letters can be reassembled into this!

In Latin 'Pater Noster' means 'Our Father'. The Greek initials 'A' and 'O' stand for Alpha and Omega, often found in Christian inscriptions. 'I am alpha and omega, the first and the last, the beginning and the end.' (Revelation 22:13)

In the Holy Land there is further evidence of early Christian devotion to places associated with Jesus himself. There was a tradition handed on verbally from one generation to the next that a particular cave in Bethlehem and a particular tomb outside the former wall of Jerusalem were the places where Jesus was born and where he was buried. The Emperor Hadrian, who built the wall between England and Scotland, was intent on obliterating any vestiges of Christianity, as well as killing off Christians, and so he intentionally built two great pagan temples over these holy places at Bethlehem and Jerusalem. In doing this, around AD 135, he was instrumental in preserving them. Some two hundred years later, when the Emperor Constantine was converted to Christianity, his mother, the Empress Helena, had these temples pulled down and the ground beneath them excavated, and they found once again the cave and the tomb, with the place of Calvary nearby. Further excavations later revealed what has been conclusively proved to be a first-century Jewish tomb, a few feet from the tomb venerated as that of Jesus. This indicated that the latter was situated in a first-century Jewish burial ground – all of which links up with the Gospel accounts.

One Solitary Life

Christians, then, throughout the ages have centred their lives on following this man, Jesus. This is summed up in the following:

WHO IS JESUS CHRIST?

He was born in an obscure village, the child of a peasant woman.
He grew up in yet another village, where he worked in a carpenter's shop until he was thirty.
Then for three years he was an itinerant preacher.
He never wrote a book.
He never held an office.
He never had a family or owned a house.
He didn't go to college.
He never travelled more than two hundred miles from the place where he was born.
He did none of the things one usually associates with greatness.
He had no credentials but himself.
He was only thirty-three when public opinion turned against him.
His friends ran away.
He was turned over to his enemies and went through the mockery of a trial.
He was nailed to a cross between two thieves.
While he was dying his executioners gambled for his clothing, the only property he had on earth.
When he was dead he was laid in a borrowed grave through the pity of a friend.
Nineteen centuries have come and gone, and today he is the central figure of the human race, the leader of mankind's progress.

All the armies that ever marched,
all the navies that ever sailed,
all the parliaments that ever sat,
all the kings that ever reigned,
put together,
have not affected

the life of man on earth
as much as that
One Solitary Life.

After we have looked at Jesus's background and culture in the next two sections, we will see more of his life, death, Resurrection and teaching. We will see how so many have been and continue to be changed, transformed through following him:

- Francis of Assisi, who gave up status and wealth to live a life of poverty.
- Mother Teresa of Calcutta, whose concern was with the incurably ill and the dying.
- Maximilian Kolbe, who gave his life to save a married man with a family.
- Margaret Clitherow, married with a family who was martyred for her faith.

These and countless others were living witnesses to the continuing presence and power of this 'Wandering Galilean'.

✠ *Prayer for this Session and During the Week*

O most merciful Redeemer, Friend and Brother;
May I know thee more clearly,
love thee more dearly,
follow thee more nearly,
day by day.

(St Richard of Chichester, 1197–1253)

? *For Discussion*

'Who do *you* say I am?' How would you reply to this question from Jesus?

NB It is quite helpful to see some colour slides of the Holy Land at this point, if they are available.

Scripture Reading

Corinthians 1:15
Start reading Mark's Gospel.

For Further Reading

Jerusalem as Jesus Knew It by John Wilkinson (Thames & Hudson)
Why Christ by Bishop B.C. Butler (DLT)

Chapter Six
Jesus's Background: The Old Testament

We now have to look at Jesus's background. He was a Jew and was part of that great religion and culture which we know so much about through the writings contained in the Old Testament.

A Collection of Books

The most important thing to remember is that the Old Testament comprises a number of different books, compiled at different times by different authors. It is rather like taking all the books from a boy's school desk – science, poetry, drama, stories, history, mathematics and so forth – and setting a bookbinder the task of trimming them and binding them together as one volume. When you open such a book you need to know immediately whether you are reading poetry, fiction or science... It is like that with the Bible as a whole, and the Old Testament in particular.

For this reason it is inadvisable to read it from beginning to end as you would any other book. Take just any one of the books, and by reading an introduction (found in some bibles) find out something about the author and why, how and when it came to be written.

Genesis

To illustrate the complexity of the Bible, we could take as an example the first book, Genesis, meaning 'the beginnings'. At least four different authors have had a hand in the composition of this 'one' book alone, spread over a period of probably several thousand years. Genesis 2:46–3:24 is the earliest section, based on a very primitive story of creation similar to that found in some other religions. Genesis 1:1–2:4 was written very much later by an Israelite priest. He wished to show that all that God created was good. The order in which he sets it out is, of course, based on the science of the day, the world being considered flat and set on pillars beneath a hemispherical vault, in which there were small holes (the stars) and around which moved the sun and moon.

Furthermore, being a Jewish priest, he had an axe to grind in that he wished to make the point that God only worked for six days – even God refrained from doing anything on the Sabbath, and therefore so must you!

So, when we read these two different accounts we must remember that we are not reading historical or scientific truth, but hearing a religious message. The religious truth encapsulated in these chapters tells us that God is good, that God created everything, and that evil originated from 'outside' God – given the fact of freedom, from the negation of God.

Freedom

This is illustrated very well indeed by a play once written by G.K. Chesterton, *The Surprise*.

It concerns a Franciscan Friar who, while wandering among the foothills of the Pyrenees in the sixteenth century, encounters a master puppet-maker (known as the Author) who owns a complete set of puppets who act and talk just like human beings in plays written for them by the Author. The Friar is interested in the puppets and the Author agrees to let him see one of the plays.

It turns out to be a delightfully poetic little fairy-tale drama in which, as the Author points out to the friar when it is all over, there is not one evil deed. All the puppets behave themselves perfectly, and the play reaches a perfect, happy-ever-after conclusion.

So like human beings are these puppets that the Author wishes they had minds and wills of their own. At the culmination of a big semi-philosophical dialogue between the Author and the Friar, the latter works a miracle and the puppets march on to the stage as real human beings possessing free will. Then, while the Friar looks on and the Author retires in amazement to the steps of his caravan, the puppets re-enact their play; but this time there is a difference, for with free will things do not turn out as before. In fact, the original play is completely ruined and two of the characters start fighting. The Author is by this time so disturbed by the way in which the play has been ruined that he calls out to them:

'What do you think you are doing with my play? Drop it! Stop! I am coming down.'

And on this note the play ends.

The religious symbolism of the whole play is, on the surface, fairly obvious: the creation by God of man, in the first place perfect, and then, through free will, his fall.

The puppet play itself is permeated by Chesterton's philosophy of surprises: 'Blessed is he that expecteth nothing for he shall be gloriously surprised.' But the final surprise, the intervention by the Author, is of course the greatest of all, and leaves the audience with a big question mark.

The Covenant with Abraham

Later in the book of Genesis, in chapter twelve, we find God making a promise to Abraham. Abraham was 'called' by God, his name changed, and his whole way of life also altered. Of course, we do not know exactly how this happened – whether in a vision or a dream, or through some human agency. What is important is that in some way or another Abraham left his former way of life and God made a covenant with him. It was based on love and trust. (A covenant is a commitment between two people, a promise by each to do something for the other. A contract is different: it is a more legal obligation.)

Genesis, chapter fifteen, is really a summary of the whole of the Bible, and describes this covenant:

> Abraham would be the Father of a nation,
> which would have a land of its own;
> and through this land and this nation, all
> nations of the earth would find blessing.

The seed was sown! The foundation of the whole Jewish people, from which Jesus was born, was to be found in this promise to Abraham – whom we describe in one of the prayers of the Mass as 'Our father in faith'.

The Exodus

The rest of the Old Testament recounts the story of this chosen people, stemming from Abraham. The most significant event in the whole of this history is the story of how Joseph, one of a large family descended from Abraham, was rejected by his brothers, ended up in Egypt, first as a slave and then as the Pharaoh's advisor. His brothers journeyed from Israel and eventually settled in

Egypt, becoming very numerous, until some two hundred years later Moses was born.

The story of the birth of Moses is well known: how he was adopted by the Pharaoh's daughter, and, when he grew up, realising his Hebrew origins, how he finally led his people away from the Egyptian yoke of slavery.

They journeyed across the sea, dry-shod, through the desert and finally back to their own land in Palestine. To guide their lives, they adopted on the way their rule of life known as the Ten Commandments. These, together with many other rules and regulations which developed over the years, were designed to guide them in their commitment to God, Yahweh (which means, 'I am who I am').

The flight from Egypt to the Promised Land was celebrated each year by the Israelites as the feast of the Passover – we will be looking at this in more detail later with reference to the history of the Mass. We see this event now as a pointer, an image of the flight from sin, through the waters of Baptism, to a life lived in God's presence.

The Prophets

The books of the Prophets are all writings by men who tried to remind the people, when they strayed from God's law, that God was calling them back. Gradually, in many of these writings, we find mention of the promise of a Messiah who will save the people. They mostly interpreted this in the earthly sense of being saved from territorial occupation by foreign forces. He would nevertheless be 'Emmanuel' (God with us). It is worth delving into some of the writings of the prophets, especially Isaiah, Jeremiah and several of the minor prophets. They are as relevant today as they ever were.

Numbers and 'Facts'

Before we leave this very brief look at the Old Testament, we should note just two useful points to help us in our reading of it:

a) In both the Old Testament and the New Testament we find various numbers mentioned in relation to different happenings. Some numbers were considered to be sacred and more important than others, and were used to express certain values. For example, seven and twelve stood for perfection, completion and holiness, forty meant a long time, a generation; and multiples of these numbers indicated an extremely long time, distance.
b) Storytelling techniques were often used and were commonly accepted at the time. These were fabricated explanations of an existing fact. For example, it might be said that the Cotswolds were caused by a giant mole throwing up earth many years ago. This is not meant to be a deliberate attempt to trick us, but merely gives a fanciful explanation for the origin of the Cotswold hills. Read Genesis 19:30–38.

The Old Testament, then, is the story of a people chosen by God. Many times they drifted off or deliberately turned away from Yahweh and were badly influenced by some of their neighbours.

Nevertheless, they gradually became a people of whom some would be utterly faithful until finally, through a young Jewish girl, Mary, a Saviour, the Messiah, Jesus, was born.

✠ *Prayer for this Session and During the Week*

O gracious and holy Father,
give us wisdom to perceive thee,
intelligence to understand thee,
diligence to seek thee,
patience to wait for thee,
eyes to behold thee,
a heart to meditate upon thee,
and a life to proclaim thee;
through the power of the Spirit of Jesus Christ our Lord.

(St Benedict, 480–543)

? *For Discussion*

Can you see any aspect of the story of God's chosen people in the Old Testament reflected in your own life?

What examples can you find in the Old Testament of poetry, science, stories, theology, history and so on?

Scripture Reading

Genesis 11:1–9; 32:23–33

Browse through the Old Testament and notice the whereabouts of the books and the different styles of writing.

For Further Reading

The Surprise by G.K. Chesterton

Chapter Seven

The Witness of the Early Christians: The New Testament

An understanding of the New Testament is enhanced greatly by the appreciation of the Old Testament and of the history and customs of the Jewish people. We have already seen that their story is, very largely, our own personal story in response to God's call and God's love. The New Testament tells us of the manifestation of God's love in Jesus Christ. It is *not* a life of Christ, although from its writings we can piece together some of the main events in his life. The four Gospels (the word means 'good news') are really summaries of the teaching of the early Church, taken from different angles. In his Gospel, John writes: 'There was much else that Jesus did; if it were written down in detail, I do not suppose the world itself would hold all the books that would be written.' (John 21:25)

The whole of the Bible, but the New Testament in particular, is essentially the book of the Church. The Church, the gathering of believers around Jesus, came first. The Gospels and the letters of some of the early followers of Jesus, which comprise most of the New Testament, are writings governed by the circumstances and situation of the writer. They are the product of the early Christian communities, and hence tell us something about that early community, and how it centred its life and faith on the Risen Lord.

Matthew's Gospel

The Gospel according to Matthew was written by one of the twelve Apostles – the inner circle. Matthew was a tax collector, an unpopular figure, as his job was to collect taxes for the occupying Roman authorities. He was also a Jew and was intent on convincing his fellow Jews that the long-awaited Messiah had come. Hence his Gospel is punctuated with frequent quotations from prophecies to this effect, taken from the Jewish writings in the Old Testament. 'And this was to fulfil the prophecy...' is an often repeated phrase in his Gospel.

John's Gospel

John was also an Apostle, but he wrote his Gospel after many years of living the life of a Christian. He was a teenager when called by Jesus, but lived to be an old man, and it was then that he set down many of his eyewitness memories of the life and ministry of Jesus. Thus we come very close indeed to the events recounted when we read John's Gospel.

Luke's Gospel

Luke and Mark were not quite so closely associated with Jesus. However, Luke is a very methodical writer and he tells us that he has talked to many eyewitnesses and then, from their testimony, has assembled his Gospel, together with what is usually called the Acts of the Apostles. This latter is a misnomer. It is really volume two of Luke's work. It is possible that he wrote more, but if he did it is now lost to us. Luke's Gospel might be described as volume one, and takes us to Jerusalem and the coming of the Holy Spirit; whereas volume two, the Acts, begins at Jerusalem (the

Jewish centre) and takes us to Rome (the centre of the pagan world).

Mark's Gospel

Mark was probably a disciple of Peter's, and there is evidence to show that the structure of his Gospel follows similar lines to the accounts of Peter's first sermons set out in the Acts. Mark's is the shortest of the four Gospels. It is the most concise, written in almost journalistic style. It is the easiest to read, and it is recommended that you sit down one evening and read it through from beginning to end.

Purpose of Writing

Each of the four Gospels is written with a particular purpose in mind, as we have already seen in the case of Matthew. The overall aim in all of them is to show that Jesus is the Messiah, the Son of God, the incarnation of God himself. Lesser aspects of this conviction show through according to the particular interest of the writer; for example, Luke emphasises Jesus's teaching on prayer, the place of women amongst his followers, and the power of the Holy Spirit.

Paul

The remainder of the New Testament is taken up, mainly, with thirteen letters of St Paul, as well as several originating with the Apostles – John, Peter, James and others. Paul, one of the early Jewish converts (converted from the persecution of Christians to the spread of the Christian Gospel), would travel from place to place around the Mediterranean. As a Jew, he would preach first of all in the synagogues, make some converts, and then proceed to speak to the Gentiles (the non-Jews), from whom he would find a few more believers. He would set up a small community with a leader (an elder), and then move on to do the same elsewhere. Sometimes he would have news of various of these groups of Christian converts he had set up. Sometimes the news was good, but not always. This would prompt a letter from Paul in which he would praise or reprimand, as the case might be. Examples of this may be found in Corinthians 11:2 and 17.

The Revelation

The last book included in the New Testament is the book of Revelation (or the Apocalypse). This comprises a series of visions, expressed in Old Testament imagery, which tell of the fall of Roman power, some forthcoming events in history and the final end of the world. Like some of Jesus's own words regarding similar topics, it is rather like two or three colour slides superimposed on one another – as if you were looking at a slide of your holiday on Brighton beach superimposed on one of St Paul's Cathedral, with glimpses of Uncle George's wedding twenty-five years ago showing through. All this makes it an extremely difficult book to read without careful guidance.

The Canon of Scripture

Some twenty years after the fall of Jerusalem, the Jewish leaders met at Jamnia in Israel, in AD 90, to discuss their future. One matter for discussion was which books of the Old Testament should be officially included in their book of scriptures. They decided eventually to have a smaller number of books than had already been accepted by the then growing and developing Christian Church. When the Bible came to be translated from its original languages at the time of the Reformation, the Protestants based the Old Testament books on the decision of the Jamnia meeting, whilst the Catholic Church continued with the use of the longer version which had been in use at the time of Jesus Himself. This explains some of the differences between the Protestant and Catholic Bibles.

By the third century there was general acceptance by the Church of the books to be included as authentic and 'inspired' in the collection which came to be known as the New Testament. However, the twenty-seven books to be included were not finally defined as such until the Council of Trent in 1546! The criteria for their general acceptance were based on their orthodoxy and origin; and it is through the Church that we have the guarantee of this.

✞ *Prayer for this Session and During the Week*

The Spirit lives to set us free,
walk, walk in the light
He binds us all in unity,
walk, walk in the light

Walk in the light (3)
walk in the light of the Lord

Jesus promised life to all,
the dead were wakened by His call.

He died in pain on Calvary,
to save the lost like you and me.

We know His death was not the end,
He gave His Spirit to be our friend.

By Jesus's love our wounds are healed,
the Father's kindness is revealed.

The Spirit lives in you and me,
His light will shine for all to see.

(Damian Lundy, 1978, Kevin Mayhew Ltd)

? *For Discussion*

With what passage from the New Testament are you most familiar? Why? Discuss.

Scripture Reading

If possible, read through, fairly quickly, Mark's Gospel, chapters one to thirteen.

For Further Reading

The Daily Study Bible by William Barclay (St Andrew Press)

Chapter Eight

Jesus: His Life and Death

We have taken a general look at the writings of the early followers of Jesus as collected for us in the New Testament. Now we will see what the Gospels, in particular, tell us about Jesus.

Jesus's Humanity

Jesus was, first and foremost, a man. Unless we are wholly convinced of his humanity, we can never be completely convinced of his divinity. So let us look at this for a moment. For some thirty years Jesus lived in a modest, almost poor home, and was probably indistinguishable from the other boys of Nazareth. When Mary looked out of the door of their house and called 'Jesus', more than one small boy would look up. 'Jesus' was, and is still, a popular name. It is the Greek form of the Hebrew 'Joshua', meaning 'Yahweh saves'.

One of the characteristics of being human is the painful process of learning and searching and discovering. Jesus didn't 'put on an act'. He did not know the details of his future, although he began to realise, early on, that his attitude, actions and teaching would almost certainly lead to him being put out of the way.

He experienced hunger (Matthew 4:2), thirst (John 4:7), tiredness (John 4:6), sorrow (John 11:35), anger (Mark 3:5), love (Mark 10:21), and had a sense of humour (Matthew 23:24, 7–3).

When we come to know a person well, we find we can pick out certain characteristics which distinguish that person, and thus we build up a particular image of him or her.

A typical 'gesture' Jesus seems to have had was that of casting a sweeping gaze over those gathered around him (Luke 6:10, Mark 10:23, Mark 3:34).

The emotion most frequently associated with him seems to have been that of pity and compassion (Matthew 9:36, Mark 6:34, Luke 7:13).

Apart from his healing and preaching, what we find him engaged in most of all is prayer (Luke 3:21, Mark 1:35, Luke 9:18, Matthew 14:23, Luke 9:28, Luke 11:1).

Jesus's Divinity

The disciples, and particularly the inner circle of the Apostles, gradually came to realise that whilst Jesus was completely human, he was very different, and they began to become aware that he was also truly divine, of God, God become man. This is the meaning of the word 'incarnation' – 'made flesh'. He not only claimed to be divine – many mentally disturbed people have done this – but he showed it through the whole of his life, teaching, and most of all his death and Resurrection. He was eminently sane in every way.

Jesus's Miracles

This was seen not only in his teaching, but in the miracles he performed. Many words in our English language have deteriorated in meaning, and one of these is the word 'miracle'. We describe getting through an exam, or a brilliant save at a football match as 'a miracle'. In the New

Testament two Greek words are used, one which means 'power' and the other 'sign'. For Jesus, a miracle always showed God's power and love entering a human situation and giving meaning to life.

In no way were the miracles of Jesus like tricks or extravagant displays designed to win over the crowds. They were signs of his love. There were, for example:

- Exorcisms: Mark 1:23–28.
- Healing miracles: Mark 1:40–45.
- Nature miracles: Mark 4:35–41.
- People raised from death: Mark 5:21–43.

All these examples are taken from Mark's Gospel, but there are many other cases of these different sorts of miracles in all the Gospels. Again, Mark, at the end of his Gospel, says that the Apostles, after the Resurrection, 'preached everywhere, the Lord working with them and confirming the word by the signs that accompanied it.'

This has gone on happening throughout the whole history of the Church. Miracles go on happening today. Space and time are somehow condensed and people are healed instantaneously. God also brings events together – providential happenings – highlighting his mercy and love. The miracles which have occurred at places such as Lourdes, or in the day-to-day gatherings of Christians at prayer, are happening in our own day. However, we must be careful to distinguish them from many current superstitious practices such as divination, spiritualism, astrology, crystal-gazing and so forth, which are all distortions of true religion and are, of course, to be avoided.

Jesus's Transfiguration

There were two significant moments in Jesus's ministry. There was the occasion when he was recognised by some of his followers as being divine: Peter's confession of faith (Matthew 16:13–20), and then the occasion when he was recognised by God, his Father: the transfiguration.

The first, the dialogue with Peter and the latter's affirmation of faith in Jesus, was set against the background of the then modern city of Caesarea Philippi, a place submerged in paganism.

There were no less than fourteen sites of ancient temples in the region; the ancient gods of Greece had their dwelling place there, and it was thought that Pan, the god of nature, was born there; it was the source of the River Jordan, reminiscent of some of the great things done by God for his chosen people; but, most significant of all, it was a very beautiful city set around a great white marble temple recently built by the Emperor Augustus for Herod the Great, and dedicated to the worship of Caesar. For this reason, Herod's son, who inherited it, changed its name, adding his own – Caesarea Philippi!

And so it was in the shadow of this great city with all its many associations, especially those connected with the glory and might of the Roman Empire, that Jesus posed the question: 'Who do people say I am?'

Peter, with considerable courage and faith, spoke for himself and the rest of them gathered around Jesus: 'We believe that you are the Son of God...'

H.V. Morton once wrote:

> The great white marble stones of the imperial temple have become building material for the house of an Arab sheikh.

> But Jesus Christ is still gloriously and triumphantly alive.
> The old faiths died;
> the old kingdoms fell;
> but the kingdom of the homeless Galilean
> still stands and still enlarges its borders throughout the world.

Shortly after this, a second event, the moment when God himself 'acclaimed', as it were, his Son, Jesus, was the happening known as the Transfiguration. Read Matthew 17:1–8, and similar accounts in Mark 9:2–8 and Luke 9:28–36. Jesus's appearance was changed, a foretaste of his Resurrection. Furthermore he appeared between Moses and Elijah. These two great figures of the Old Testament epitomise the law and the prophets, which both find their meeting point and culmination in Jesus. This event was really the turning point in Jesus's ministry. From then on he seems set for Jerusalem and the ultimate sacrifice of the cross, followed by the glory of his Resurrection.

Jesus's Claims

To say that Jesus is 'the Son of God' is to claim that he has a unique relationship with God. This has to be a personal discovery for each one of us. On other occasions, Jesus said: 'I and the Father are one'; 'He who sees me, sees the Father'; 'Before Abraham was, I am'; but these were in response to questions put to him by the Apostles. Jesus generally encourages others to discover him for themselves. The scribes and Pharisees reacted against him when they saw clear evidence of his divinity: 'Who is this man, talking blasphemy? Who but God alone can forgive sins?' (Luke 5:21)

And so it is with us. Our knowledge and love of him hesitates and grows. It is a knowledge and love that is helped by reading, by listening to talks, by sharing, by going to church, by reading the Gospels and so on, but most of all it comes through a personal encounter with him in the silence of our hearts.

From what we have seen, we should now realise that Jesus did not use his divinity to bypass the difficulties of his humanity. He grew and developed in wisdom and knowledge (Luke 2:52), and learned, as we do, to live as a human being. In all things he was like us, except in sin. Furthermore, it was only gradually that he became aware of the suffering and ultimate death that his mission would lead to. However, there is general agreement amongst theologians that Jesus must always have been in some way aware of his special relationship with God as Son to Father, and of his special relationship with mankind as Word from God. This awareness does not necessarily mean that he knew consciously who he was and what he was meant to do, but rather that to be Son and Word was so much a part of his very being that it coloured the whole of his life. Only as his consciousness dawned and developed would the conviction that he was God's Son and Word have grown correspondingly more articulate and clear. Beyond that we cannot say; we do not know.

Jesus's Crucifixion

His death was utterly scandalous to his followers. How could he, who had led his Apostles and so many others to a belief in his divinity, allow himself to be led off as a common criminal? It is no wonder that Peter denied him, and that nearly all the others abandoned him at the crucial moment (Mark 14:50).

Most will have experienced the death of a relative or friend. Invariably, after the death of such a person, the last events one recalls of him or her stand out vividly. It is only later that other happenings, together with oddments connected with his or her childhood are pieced together. It was like that with Jesus. The accounts of the sufferings leading to his Crucifixion are graphically recounted in the Gospels. There are slight variations in the sequence and details, but these only highlight their authenticity. If each account were absolutely identical, it would point to forgery – no two signatures of the same person are quite identical. Two different historians once described different routes for Hannibal crossing the Alps. However, the essential truth was that he did cross the Alps and arrive in Italy.

It was necessary that Jesus should give himself up willingly, a complete and perfect offering to the Father for us. It was the sign, par excellence, of love, perfect love: 'No one can have greater love than to lay down his life for his friends.' (John 15:13) If Jesus had died of a heart attack in the streets of Capernaum, then our religion would have taken on a quite different form. At the heart of our faith is the Cross, but coupled with this is, of course, his Resurrection.

✠ *Prayer for this Session and During the Week*

Lord, teach me to be generous
teach me to serve you as you deserve
to give
and not to count the cost
to fight

and not to heed the wounds
to toil
and not to seek for rest
to labour
and not to seek reward
save that of knowing
I do your most holy will.
(Prayer of St Ignatius)

? *For Discussion*

Who is Jesus to you?
What three characteristics that you may find in a Christian would you say are most Christlike?

Scripture Reading

The account of the passion and death of Jesus in any of the four Gospels.
John 10:19–21

For Further Reading

Interpreting the Miracles by R.H. Fuller (SCM Press)
The Snow Goose by Paul Gallico

Chapter Nine
Jesus: His Resurrection and the Trinity

'...if Christ has not been raised, then our preaching is without substance, and so is your faith', and all is pointless, wrote St Paul. (1 Corinthians 15:14) We have seen some of the vivid details surrounding the suffering and death of Jesus. This vividness and detail are carried on in the accounts of his Resurrection. There are slight discrepancies with regard to a few minor points, but these need not bother us: the salient and overriding fact is that the Apostles and many of the disciples experienced his presence among them subsequent to the discovery of the empty tomb.

The Nature of Jesus's Resurrection

The accounts of the Resurrection really comprise two discoveries: the empty tomb and his appearances. The empty tomb, of itself, is insufficient, but when this is followed by many occasions when he appeared to his followers, then we have clear evidence of his 'survival'. Jesus's Resurrection in no way implies the reanimation of his body as it was up to his Crucifixion. In the case of Lazarus, his friend, who was brought back to life after several days in the tomb (John 11:1–44), or that of the son of the widow of Nain (Luke 7:11), it was the bringing back to life of a corpse. In the case of Jesus, it was an event of a different kind. His body was changed, transformed, glorified, so much so that at first he was not recognised (Luke 24:13–35; John 21:1–8; John 20:11–18). In some way he was different. It was a completely new and unique event, and, as with many other elements of belief, there are pointers to its reality and truth, but ultimately we have to make a leap of faith.

No one saw the Resurrection actually take place, and the writers of the Gospels were sceptical at first. They emphasised the fact that it was some women who first discovered the empty tomb. The word of a woman in those days was not to be relied on... Perhaps only now is the Church beginning to catch up on the events of the first Resurrection morning in that respect.

Jesus's Appearances

Furthermore, Jesus appeared in the ordinary everyday circumstances of life: whilst having a meal, in a garden, whilst fishing, on a journey and so forth. They were extraordinary appearances in ordinary situations. Suddenly he would be there. It was as if his thought had complete and total power over his risen body. In a sense they were one. It was a little like you sitting in your chair now, but instantaneously, in your mind, being at home in your bedroom, picturing the position of the bed, the wardrobe, the window and so on, while in fact you continue to be seated where you are. With a glorified body you would actually be where your thought conveyed you.

Jesus appeared in this way for a short time. It was a transitional state. At first his followers failed to recognise him, because in some mysterious way he was different; nevertheless they came to see through the outward appearance.

One of Agatha Christie's books tells the story of a character, who turns out to be the murderer, who was a superb actor. He disguised himself very successfully in all sorts of different roles: as a hospital attendant, a butcher's delivery man, a doctor, a waiter in a restaurant. Each time he looked different. However, it became known that he had a particular habit, of which he wasn't conscious, of playing with the breadcrumbs whilst he was eating – and it was this that finally gave him away. He was recognised through a very ordinary little habit. It was somewhat like this with the Risen Lord. He was recognised by the tone of his voice when he said, 'Mary', in the garden, by the breaking of the bread and so on.

These transitional appearances of Jesus were to prepare his followers to recognise him in their fellow human beings, especially those in need (Matthew 25:31–46), and in the Eucharist (John 6:32–71). Both of these will be dealt with in subsequent sessions.

The Resurrection, then, was a unique event. It was a challenge to faith. It is at the very centre of faith. It is not Jesus's teaching, or his miracles, or even the way he died that causes us to believe in him. It is his Resurrection from death that is at the very heart of faith. Let us consider an example of this.

Medieval artists often saw the transformation of the caterpillar into a butterfly as a reminder of the Resurrection, and so, on the edge of some ancient stained-glass windows you can see the image of a butterfly.

This, of course, is an inadequate image, as the very nature of the risen body of Jesus was different, and his appearances were a transition towards the invisible reality of the next life: to help us to believe in things unseen.

After the experience of the Resurrection, and especially subsequent to being filled and fired with enthusiasm and love at Pentecost, the coming of the Holy Spirit, the

Apostles and disciples became very different and could not stop talking about these two events in the life of Jesus: his death and Resurrection.

The Paschal Mystery

Acts 2:22–24 hold the essence of Peter's preaching:

> 'Men of Israel, listen to what I am going to say: Jesus the Nazarene was a man commended to you by God by the miracles and portents and signs that God worked through him when he was among you, as you know. This man, who was put into your power by the deliberate intention and foreknowledge of God, you took and had crucified and killed by men outside the Law. But God raised him to life...'

This is absolutely central to our faith as Christians. Throughout our lives, and indeed daily, we are called to live out this pattern of 'dying' and 'rising'. In any act of unselfish love, or concern and caring for another person, there is a death to the self and, through that, a rising to new life. This attains its peak and perfection in the death and Resurrection of Jesus. In the Church we are caught up, through our baptism, into the community of people who are called by God to live this out, and thus be transformed ourselves as well as being the instruments of transformation of the world around us. Gerald O'Collins has expressed this well:

> The first Easter began the work of finally bringing our universe home to its ultimate destiny. God did not discard Jesus's earthly corpse, but mysteriously raised and transfigured it so as to reveal what lies ahead for human beings and their world. In brief, the

> empty tomb is God's radical sign that redemption is not an escape to a better world but an extraordinary transformation of this world.

This makes the death and Resurrection of Jesus, the Paschal Mystery, completely relevant to us today. All this is gathered into our Easter liturgy towards which this journey in faith leads us. It does not stop at the Crucifixion (we are not 'Good Friday' Christians!), but goes on to the Resurrection (we are 'Easter' people!), and our cry is 'Alleluia' – Praise to God: Christ is risen.

The Trinity

Jesus's Resurrection and hence his divinity, coupled with his promise to give to his followers the gift of the Holy Spirit, his Spirit of love, leads us immediately to consider our belief in the Trinity. God is three, yet God is one. What a paradox!

A Muslim would say: 'Why do you complicate things? God is one! How can there be three persons in one God?' And yet Jesus has revealed this to us.

In his final instructions to his Apostles, he tells them: 'Go, therefore, make disciples of all nations; baptise them in the name of the Father and of the Son and of the Holy Spirit...' (Matthew 28:19)

THE CREATIVE ACT

Perhaps we can look at it in this way – not in an attempt to explain the Trinity, but rather to show that it is not quite so absurd as it may appear at first. Imagine you are an artist – a very good one – and you intend painting a picture of a lake, mountains, a boat and fishermen on the lake, the sun shining in a particular direction and so forth. As a good artist you will think carefully of the design of your picture.

It will exist as an *idea* in your mind. Perhaps you will tell others about this picture you are going to paint. You then get out your paints and transpose your idea on to the canvas, and if you are a very good artist, what appears on the canvas will be the 'incarnation' of the idea in your mind – the idea becomes visible, tangible and so on. This, one might term the *action*. Then you stand back and are pleased with what you have done. You like it. Could we use a stronger word? You *love* it, and you hope others will too.

Here we have three 'aspects' of this one picture: the idea, the incarnation of the idea and the love, the bond between the two. Now this 'pattern' applies to everything we do. If I go home to prepare supper, I think first of what I am going to do, secondly, I do it, and, if I do it as well as I am able, I am pleased with what I have done.

Some of our actions are done more or less automatically, without thought. However, somewhere along the line, perhaps a long time ago, there was this threefold pattern of idea, action and love. For example, in driving a car, at some point you had to think how and when to put the clutch in, but after a time it becomes automatic. The same applies to walking and many other actions.

Going back to the creative act (painting the picture, writing a letter, work and so on), we see here, most of all, pointers to the heavenly Trinity which is God. God, the Father, the complete and perfect 'idea', who revealed something of himself in different religions and particularly, as we have seen, to the Jewish people. God, the Son, the 'idea' become flesh, God-made-man: now we can 'see' God incarnate. And, finally, the love between the two, which proceeds from the Father and the Son, is the Holy Spirit.

I would repeat that what I have described is a *pointer* to the Trinity, and *not* an explanation of it. It remains a mystery. What I have tried to show is that in looking at ourselves and the way our own minds function, we can see some sort of dim reflection of God, the Trinity. It is in this sense that the writer of the book of Genesis says that man is made in the image of God.

Thus we see that the Christian teaching about the Trinity evolves directly from Jesus's claim to be divine, God-made-man, God incarnate, and this itself is indicated and shown by his Resurrection from the dead. Jesus, in his farewell discourse to his Apostles, promises them that he will ask the Father '...and he will give you another Paraclete [or protector], to be with you for ever, the Spirit of truth...' (John 14:16)

The following story, which comes from India, might be termed an allegory of much of what we have been considering.

BAMBOO

Once upon a time, in the heart of the western kingdom, lay a beautiful garden. And there, in the cool of the day, was the master of the garden, who went for a walk. Of all the dwellers of the garden, the most beautiful and beloved was a gracious and noble Bamboo. Year after year, Bamboo grew yet more beautiful and gracious. He was conscious of his master's love and watchful delight, yet he was modest and in all things gentle.

Often, when Wind came to revel in the garden, Bamboo would throw aside his dignity. He would dance and sway merrily, tossing and leaping and bowing in joyous abandon. He would lead the great dance of the garden which most delighted his master's heart.

One day the master drew near to look at his Bamboo with eyes of curious expectancy. And Bamboo, in a passion of love, bowed his great head to the ground in joyful greeting. The master spoke:

'Bamboo, I would use you.'

Bamboo flung his head to the sky in utter delight. The day of days had been growing hour by hour, the day in which he would find his completion and destiny! His voice came low:

'Master, I am ready, use me as you want.'

'Bamboo,' said the master, his voice grave, 'I would be obliged to take you and cut you down.'

A trembling of great horror shook Bamboo. 'Cut... me... down? Me, whom you, master, have made the most beautiful in all of your garden? To cut me down, ah, not that, not that. Use me for your job, oh master, but cut me not down.'

'Beloved Bamboo...' The master's voice grew graver still. 'If I do not cut you down, then I cannot use you.'

The garden grew still. Wind held her breath. Bamboo slowly bent his proud and glorious head. There came a whisper.

'Master, if you cannot use me unless you cut me down, then do your will and cut.'

'Bamboo, beloved Bamboo, I would cut your leaves and branches from you also.'

'Master, master, spare me. Cut me down and lay my beauty in the dust, but would you take from me my leaves and branches also?'

'Bamboo, alas! If I do not cut them away, I cannot use you.'

The sun hid her face. A listening butterfly glided fearfully away. Bamboo shivered in terrible expectancy, whispering low, 'Master, cut away.'

'Bamboo, Bamboo, I would divide you in two and cut out your heart, for if I do not cut so, I cannot use you.'

'Master, master, then cut and divide.'

So the master of the garden took Bamboo and cut him down and hacked off his branches and stripped off his leaves and divided him in two and cut out his heart, and, lifting him gently, carried him to where there was a spring of fresh, sparkling water in the midst of the master's dry fields. Then, putting down one end of broken Bamboo into the spring, and the other end into the water channel in his field, the master laid down gently his beloved Bamboo.

The spring sang welcome. The clear sparkling water raced joyously down the channel of Bamboo's torn body into the waiting fields. Then the rice was planted and the days went by. The shoots grew. The harvest came. In that day was Bamboo, once so glorious in his stately beauty, yet more glorious in his brokenness and humility.

For in his beauty he was life abundant. But in his brokenness he became a channel of abundant life to his master's world.

(Origin unknown)

✞ *Prayer for this Session and During the Week*

Lord Jesus,
I give you my hands to do your work.
I give you my feet to go your way.

I give you my eyes to see as you do.
I give you my tongue to speak your words.
I give you my mind that you may think in me.
I give you my spirit that you may pray in me.
Above all, I give you my heart that you may love in me
your Father and all mankind.
I give you my whole self that you may grow in me,
so that it is you, Lord Jesus,
who live and work and pray in me.
Amen.

(Grail prayer)

? *For Discussion*

What do you recall most vividly about the Resurrection of Jesus? Why?

What 'images' of God have you had in the past?

Scripture Reading

The Resurrection narratives in the final chapters of each of the four Gospels.

1 Corinthians 15:1–19

Luke 20:27–40

For Further Reading

The Mind of the Maker by Dorothy Sayers

Chapter Ten
The Church Founded by Jesus: The People of God

Jesus did not sit down and write a book. He gathered together a very mixed and unlikely group of people and to some of these, the twelve Apostles, he gave a particular charge to go out and spread the Good News that he had taught them. Furthermore, he guaranteed that they would be guided through the power of God's love, the Holy Spirit.

The Power of the Holy Spirit

I suppose if you or I were to manage to get into some steel factory in Sheffield, or to the London docks, and were to approach any of the chaps there at random, tell them to pack up what they were doing and just come along, that you would give them something else to do, without telling them what it was, and suggesting that there would be little or no money in it anyway, then their reaction would be, to put it bluntly, to get lost!

And yet, you know, that is precisely what Christ did, and the reaction wasn't to avoid him or take no notice of him because he was mad. They followed him... There must have been something simply astounding about Our Lord... his personality, his dignity. After all, they realised later that he was the perfection of manhood, and later still, that he was God himself come on this earth of ours...

They followed him, leaving their boats, their nets, their livelihood. They became 'apostles', a word which means an envoy, one sent out with authority.

Just as Mary received the gift of God's Spirit at the announcement of Jesus's conception and set off to share the good news with her cousin, Elizabeth, so the Apostles also were filled with the gift of that same Spirit, to go out and spread the Good News to the ends of the known world.

Fifty days after the Resurrection, the Apostles were gathered together, with Mary and some of the other women, waiting in prayer, as Jesus had commanded them (Acts 1:12–14). In a mysterious and wonderful manner they were filled with the Holy Spirit (Acts 2:1–13), they were caught up in that love existing between the Father and the Son.

This gift of the Spirit formed the early Church and continues to form the Church today. Following Jesus Christ always involves spreading his message, his life and his love. Christians can never be like the little girl who was given a coronation mug and immediately said, 'I'm going to keep it to put my false teeth in!'

The First Christians

We have a brief sketch of the life of the very first Christians in Acts 2:42–47. It seems to have been a semi-monastic style of living, which later became adapted to the situation and culture of the surrounding peoples. Authority in these early communities soon became apparent. St Paul, after setting up a community of convert Jews and Gentiles (converted pagans), and before journeying on to another town, appointed an elder to be in charge. Sometimes things went wrong, and he himself had to intervene to correct an abuse. On one occasion there developed a deep division between the Christians of Jewish origin and those of Gentile background. The former insisted that certain Jewish customs, such as circumcision, be adhered to by the Gentiles as well. A great gathering, the first council of the Church, was held at Jerusalem around AD 48 for the matter to be resolved. We read in Acts 15:1–31 that, 'It has been decided by the Holy Spirit, and by ourselves...' A decision was arrived at. Circumcision was not essential!

Determining the Scriptures

A further most important matter was settled at two later councils of the Church: the Council of Hippo in AD 393 and that of Carthage in AD 397. Up to that time there were over one hundred and ten books of the Old and New Testaments in circulation. The Church met to determine which were inspired and which were not. We have seen already how this affected the Old Testament. There were also various other gospels and letters in circulation amongst Christians. We only know through the authority of the Church which scriptures we can rely on. St Augustine the Great, who was present at the council, wrote, 'I would not believe the Gospel unless moved thereto by the authority of the Church!'

Images of the Church

The Church was to be the sign and sacrament of God's presence in the world. It comprises the people of God, and in the Gospels and the letters of St Paul, various aspects of the Church are highlighted by comparisons: with a sheepfold, a net cast into the sea, a building; a human body with its many gifts, a loving spouse, a tree that grows and develops from a tiny seed and so on. Some of the examples given point to the presence of the Kingdom within the individual, whilst others emphasise its presence in the world – the Body of the Church. Sometimes the parables of the Kingdom can be interpreted in both ways. This is not the place to give an exegesis of these passages, but the above points should be borne in mind.

Belonging to the Church

A person can belong to the visible Church in various ways. These are set out in the Vatican II document on the Church, and they range from those who are baptised and who believe in the revelation of God through Jesus Christ within the context of the Church, to those who, through no fault of their own, do not know God, but who sincerely try to lead a good life as they understand it.

Marks of the Church

Early in its history four clear 'marks' were seen to characterise the Church: it was to be One, Holy, Catholic and Apostolic:

- *One*: in the sense that there is a unity of belief on essential matters; a desire to follow the guidance of the Church in questions of morality; and a unity of worship centred on the Mass and the Sacraments. This, however, must not be confused with uniformity. Unity stems from the authority we find in the Church, and this will be dealt with in the next session.
- *Holy*: the Church is holy, but not in the sense that all its members are holy – far from it! It is very much like the fisherman's net, gathering in all sorts and conditions of people, good, bad and indifferent. The holiness of the Church stems from its founder, Jesus, and his special presence in and through the Church. Furthermore, the

Church's teaching is a holy teaching, enabling us, if we follow it, to become holy, whole, and many have – witness the saints, known and unnamed.

Infallible or not – I'm afraid His Holiness won't be helping you pick your lottery numbers!

- *Catholic*: this word means 'universal'. The Church is for all people of all time. 'Go and teach all nations...' said Jesus. It is a teaching that is available to men and women of all countries, colours, nationalities and cultures and of all ages. No one is excluded, and it is perhaps the only organisation that gathers together, week after week, in our town parishes, such a motley array of different folk, mixing up social classes, ethnic backgrounds and political creeds.
- *Apostolic*: the Church, through its leadership in the bishops, and their ordination through the laying on of hands, can be traced back to the time of the Apostles, and hence to Jesus himself. It is also apostolic in the sense that it teaches essentially the same doctrine and

way of life as taught by the early Church and by Jesus himself. However, as we shall see again later when looking at the Sacraments, that teaching was very much like a seed sown in the ground and allowed to grow and develop. Its onward forms change over the centuries whilst, in essence, remaining the same.

Each One Different

We have within us all that is necessary to become members, in the fullest sense, of the Church – each has something different to offer. This is illustrated in the following story, told by Anthony de Mello.

A woman in a village was surprised to find a fairly well-dressed stranger at her door asking for something to eat. 'I'm sorry,' she said. 'I have nothing in the house right now.'

'Not to worry,' said the amiable stranger. 'I have a soup stone in this satchel of mine; if you will let me put it in a pot of boiling water I'll make the most delicious soup in the world. A very large pot, please.'

The woman was curious. She put the pot on the fire and whispered the secret of the soup stone to a neighbour. By the time the water began to boil, all the neighbours had gathered to see the stranger and his soup stone.

The stranger dropped the stone into the water, then tasted a teaspoonful with relish and exclaimed, 'Ah, delicious! All it needs is some potatoes.'

'I have potatoes in my kitchen,' shouted one woman. In a few minutes she was back with a large quantity of sliced potatoes that were thrown into the pot.

Then the stranger tasted the brew again. 'Excellent!' he said, but added wistfully, 'If we only had some meat, this would become a tasty stew.'

Another housewife rushed home to bring some meat which the stranger accepted graciously and flung into the pot. When he tasted the broth again he rolled his eyes heavenwards and said, 'Ah, tasty! If we had some vegetables it would be perfect, absolutely perfect.'

One of the neighbours rushed off home and returned with a basketful of carrots and onions. After these had been thrown in too and the stranger tasted the mixture, he said in voice of command, 'Salt and sauce.'

'Right here,' said the housewife.

Then came another command: 'Bowls for everyone.'

People rushed to their homes in search of bowls. Some even brought back bread and fruit.

Then they all sat down to a delicious meal while the stranger handed out large helpings of his incredible soup.

Everyone felt strangely happy as they laughed and talked and shared their very first common meal. In the middle of the merriment the stranger quietly slipped away, leaving behind the miraculous soup stone that they could use any time they wanted to make the loveliest soup in the world.

☩ *Prayers for this Session and During the Week*

THE NICENE CREED

We believe in one God, the Father, the Almighty, maker of heaven and earth, of all that is, seen and unseen.

We believe in one Lord, Jesus Christ, the only Son of God, eternally begotten of the Father, God from God, Light from Light, true God from true God, begotten, not made, of one Being with the Father. Through Him all things were made. For us men and for our salvation he came down from heaven: [all bow] by the power of the Holy Spirit he became incarnate from the Virgin Mary, and was made man. For our sake He was crucified under Pontius Pilate; he suffered death and was buried. On the third day he rose again in accordance with the Scriptures; he ascended into heaven and is seated at the right hand of the Father. He will come again in glory to judge the living and the dead, and his kingdom will have no end. We believe in the Holy Spirit, the Lord, the giver of life, who proceeds from the Father and the Son. With the Father and the Son he is worshipped and glorified. He has spoken through the Prophets. We believe in one holy catholic and apostolic Church. We acknowledge one baptism for the forgiveness of sins. We look for the resurrection of the dead, and the life of the world to come. Amen.

HAIL MARY

Hail, Mary, full of grace, the Lord is with thee: blessed art thou among women, and blessed is the fruit of thy womb, Jesus. Holy Mary, Mother of God, pray for us sinners, now, and at the hour of our death. Amen.

? *For Discussion*

From what you have experienced already of the Catholic Church, can you see in her the four 'marks' of the Church – one, holy, catholic and apostolic?

Scripture Reading

1 Corinthians 12

For Further Reading

The Document of Vatican II on 'The Church'

Chapter Eleven
The Church: Its Authority and Organisation; Mary, its First Member

We have seen that the Catholic Church was founded by Jesus and has carried on his teaching down the ages. This could not happen without some guarantee of authority, some binding authority. This is perhaps a concept that many fight shy of today. However, Jesus spoke with authority (Mark 1:22), and it was precisely this that repelled some whilst it attracted others. Moreover, we see how he gave this same authority to his 'inner circle' of followers, the Apostles. 'As you [Father] sent me into the world, I have sent them into the world.' (John 17:18) 'Go out to the whole world; proclaim the Gospel to all creation.' (Mark 16:15) This was his commission to the whole group of Apostles. Furthermore, he singled out one for the particular task of holding them together and being their leader.

Simon Peter

When Jesus first gathered the Apostles around him, he spoke to Simon and changed his name. He gave him a sort of nickname. Nicknames usually highlight a particular trait in a person's character or appearance. In the case of Simon, it didn't. In fact it was the reverse. When Andrew, Simon's brother, took him to Jesus, he looked at him and said, 'You are Simon son of John; you are to be called Cephas', which means rock. (John 1:42) We also find that Simon is mentioned no less than one hundred and ninety times in the Gospels and Acts, whilst St John, who comes next, is mentioned only twenty-nine times! Furthermore, most of the references to Simon Peter are the result of Jesus turning to him or bringing him forward, and are not founded upon his own initiative.

Later, after Simon's profession of faith in Jesus, the latter turned to him and said, 'You are Cephas, and on this cephas I will build my Church...' (Matthew 16:18) In English we lose the full impact of this, as the name 'Peter' is not the word for 'rock'. In Aramaic (which Jesus spoke), as well as some other languages – for example, Greek and French – the two words are the same, and the importance of what Jesus was saying comes over more clearly.

Authority

In the documents relating to the history of the early Church, there are clear references to the leadership role of Peter and of his successors as bishops of Rome. Bishops, as successors to the Apostles, have a leadership role over a particular territory (priests are their aides), but in the case of Peter's successors, we find the role of confirming and strengthening the brethren vested in him alone. Again, the realisation of what is involved in Jesus's words to Peter, as well as to the Apostles as a group, and to their successors, has been gradually unfolding over the ages:

> ...whatever you bind on earth will be bound in heaven; whatever you loose on earth will be loosed in heaven.
>
> (Matthew 16:19)

Councils

Throughout the history of the Church, different problems have arisen which have necessitated a gathering of the bishops in what is called a council of the Church, in order to agree on the right solution according to the mind of Christ. The first major problem, as we have seen, arose some fifteen years after the Resurrection, regarding Gentile (i.e. pagan) and Jewish converts to the Church. And over the centuries, there have been other general councils of the Church, mostly to resolve some question of faith or morals.

Recent years, 1963–5, have witnessed Vatican Council II, through which a lot of 'spring-cleaning' was done. There was a greater opening up to the world and a clearer view of what is essential in our faith through the clearing out of some of the unnecessary accretions. This was seen particularly in the Church's liturgy, or worship. It also clarified the place of the bishops as a group, the importance of them working together for the whole Church and taking the message of Christ to all. It is in this sense that they are known as the college of bishops.

Infallibility

Prior to this council, there was another in 1870, which clarified the position of Peter, as the head, and his successors as bishops of Rome. Penetrating the full importance of Jesus's words to Peter, and the way this had worked out in history, the Church declared that when Peter's successors (the Popes) defined something with regard to faith or morals (what we believed and how that faith was to be put into practice), then they were prevented by the Holy Spirit from falling into error. It put a somewhat negative angle on authority. In no way did it state that everything the Pope said was to be seen in this category of being 'infallible'. Nor did it mean that the Pope could wake up one fine morning and decide to make an infallible pronouncement. Furthermore, the Pope had to be seen to be teaching the whole Church, and not just a group of Italian housewives or Australian workers! It has to be the crystallisation of what was already believed in by the Church as a whole. Thus there is always a great deal of consultation prior to any pronouncement. Finally, this way of exercising authority in the Church is fairly rare: it has been used by the Popes less than ten times in two thousand years. It applies also, of course, to whatever the bishops as a whole agree on.

Because we believe in the guidance of the Holy Spirit in the Church, we also show great respect for the ordinary teaching of the Church, even though it may not come under the strict umbrella of 'infallibility'. We all need this leadership, guidance and help in living out our Christian lives.

This whole question of authority and freedom from error has to be seen in the context of the faith of the whole Church. The following statement of the bishops at Vatican II states this very clearly:

> The body of the faithful as a whole, anointed as they are by the Holy One, (1 John 2:20–27) cannot err in matters of belief. Thanks to a supernatural sense of the faith which characterises the people as a whole, it manifests this unerring quality when, 'from the bishops down to the last member of the laity', it shows universal agreement in matters of faith and morals...
>
> (Lumen Gentium 12)

The bishops as a whole, and the Pope in particular, as we have already seen, are there to shepherd the flock clearly and authoritatively.

The First Follower of Jesus: Mother of God and Mother of the Church

Mary, the mother of Jesus, was the first follower of her son. She was the first member of the Church, and she was the greatest – totally human, chosen of all the women who have ever lived, to be the mother of the God-man. Because of this, at the Vatican Council II it was agreed to devote a whole section to Mary in the document on the Church. We cannot rate her highly enough amongst us humans, but we always have to remember that there is an infinite difference between her and her son, who was divine. It is true that we find among some Catholics an exaggerated devotion to her. Cardinal Newman once said that a people's religion is always a corrupt religion.

The teaching of the Church is simply that Mary was chosen to have the highest vocation of all, and she was singled out for this by being free from any 'stain' of rebellion against God (original sin). Then, finally, because of her totally good life, she attained, in both body and soul, the glory and peace of eternal life in heaven with her son. In technical terms those two beliefs are known as her *Immaculate Conception* and her *Assumption.* She was God's choice, but she still had the freedom to say 'no' at the *Annunciation*, when she in fact gave the perfect response: '...let it happen to me as you have said.' (Luke 1:38) In this, she conformed exactly to God's plan for her.

After the Resurrection and Ascension of her son, Mary, as we have seen, was with the Apostles and others, probably in the same upper room in which the Last Supper had been celebrated. She was there, just as she had been at the Last Supper, when, as the mother, she would have lit the lamps for the Passover. When the Apostles looked at her they would have been reminded in a striking way of Jesus, for he had taken the whole of his humanity from his mother, and the strong facial likeness must have been very striking – much more so than is normally the case between son and mother.

So, then, we do not *worship* Mary. We honour her and venerate her as the greatest of the saints because God chose her of all women who have ever lived and who ever will live on this earth, to be his mother. As at Cana, on the occasion of Jesus's first miracle of changing water into wine (itself a pointer to the Eucharist), Mary continues to point to her son: 'Do whatever he tells you.' (John 2:5) This is the simple message which comes through in the various apparitions of Our Lady in past years, but it becomes a more urgent message in our own day: 'Do whatever he tells you.'

♱ *Prayers for this Session and During the Week*

THE MAGNIFICAT

My soul proclaims
the greatness of the Lord
and my spirit rejoices
in God my Saviour
because he has looked upon
the humiliation of his servant
Yes, from now onwards
all generations will call me blessed,
for the almighty
has done great things for me.
Holy is his name
and his faithful love extends age after age
to those who fear him.

He has used the power of his arm,
he has routed the arrogant of heart.
He has pulled down princes
from their thrones
and raised high the lowly.
He has filled the starving with good things,
sent the rich away empty.
He has come to the help
of Israel his servant,
mindful of his faithful love
– according to the promise
he made to our ancestors –
of his mercy to Abraham
and to his descendants for ever.

THE MEMORARE

Remember, O most loving Virgin Mary, that
it is a thing unheard of, that anyone ever had
recourse to your protection, implored your

help, or sought your intercession,
and was left forsaken.

Filled therefore with confidence in your
goodness I fly to you, O Mother,
Virgin of virgins.

To you I come, before you I stand, a
sorrowful sinner. Despise not my poor
words, O Mother of the Word of God, but
graciously hear and grant my prayer.

Amen.

A JOYFUL DECADE OF THE ROSARY:
THE ANNUNCIATION

? *For Discussion*

How do you react to authority in your daily life and in the Church?
What do you think of the place given to Mary in the Church?

Scripture Reading

Luke 1:1–56
John 2:1–11
Matthew 16:13–20

For Further Reading

The Document of Vatican II on 'The Church'
One Lord One Faith by Vernon Johnson

Chapter Twelve
The Basis of Our Life of Faith: Prayer

In one of the APPETISER sessions we looked at some aspects of prayer in a general way. Now is the time to consider prayer in greater detail. We are dealing with the subject at this juncture, before we look at the sacraments, as prayer forms the basis of all else that we do, both 'in church' as well as outside.

Jesus at Prayer

Jesus knew this, and we know from the Gospels that he spent much time communing with his Heavenly Father. Luke, particularly, underlines it in his Gospel. Read especially Luke 3:21; 4:1–13; 4:42; 5:16; 6:12; 9:59; 22:41–46; 23:34; and 23:46. Similar mention is found in both Mark and Matthew's Gospels, with further insight to Jesus's prayer in John's Gospel, which shows more clearly the deep inner union of Jesus with God, his Father.

There is a game I remember playing years ago ('How, When, Where and Why?'), in which one person goes out of the room whilst the others decide on some object, event... anything. The person then comes in and goes around the circle, asking '*How* one liked it?', and then 'When?', 'Where?' and 'Why?' In the reverse order this forms a good basis for looking at prayer.

Why Do We Pray?

One might equally ask the question 'Why do we love?', for prayer is an attitude of loving, an attentiveness of the loved one to the lover. St Thérèse of Lisieux describes prayer as 'an aspiration of the heart, a humble glance towards heaven, a cry of gratitude and of love whether it be in a time of trial or of joy. It is in a word something elevated and supernatural which fills the soul and unites it with God.' In whatever form it takes, prayer is communication between God and us. To be fully human, we have to pray: that spiritual part of ourselves, the essential 'me', has to breathe.

Where Should We Pray?

The short answer to that is: anywhere! We can pray out in the country, at work, whilst walking or travelling, at home, perhaps at a specially prepared 'prayer place', or in church.

God's presence is, first and foremost, within us, and so we can be in touch with him anywhere and at any time. There's the story of the man who was on his knees searching for something.

His friend came up and said, 'What are you looking for?'

'My key – I've lost it.'

Both men got on their knees to search for the lost key. After a while the friend said, 'Where did you lose it?'

'At home,' was the reply.

'Good Lord! Then why are you searching for it here?'

'Because there's more light here,' replied the man.

It is no good searching for God in holy places, like the church, if we've lost him in our hearts. The way we pray at Mass must grow out of our private prayer, our personal communing with him.

For this personal, private prayer, our room at home is usually the best place. However, for married people, this can sometimes be the living room, and can include other members of the family and become a time of shared prayer. This is certainly a good situation in which to introduce children to prayer, and growth in faith. At the meal-table, before and after the meal, can also be an appropriate moment for turning to God in trust, love and thanksgiving.

Visual aids, like a lighted candle, some holy water, the picture or statue of a saint, a simple crucifix and suchlike can all help to centre the heart and mind on the things of God.

When Should We Pray?

Whatever we are doing and wherever we are, we still have that essential relationship with God who loves us, totally and unchangingly, and so at any time of the day or night we can, for a moment, *be aware* of God's presence and remind ourselves of his love. This can be a silent awareness, or, mentally, expressed in words.

It is good, however, to set aside a certain length of time for prayer to the exclusion of all else: morning and evening each day, and once a week on a Sunday (or Saturday evening) to gather together with others of the faith to celebrate Mass, the great act of praise, thanksgiving, repentance and petition that we make to God as we are caught up in the offering of Jesus to his Father.

The person who comes to Mass in order to say his own private and favourite devotions, hasn't grasped the meaning of the Mass and public worship at all. One is reminded of the story of the four year old girl who was taken to Mass for the first time, and, at the very outset, when everybody was kneeling down, she showed the usual disposition to talk.

'Hush,' said her mother, 'they are going to pray now.'

'What,' said the little girl, 'with all their clothes on?'

If we love, we must find time to love. There will be times when we are exhausted, worn out with responsibilities and worries, when we are overworked and perhaps unwell: we then have to force ourselves to 'waste time' with God.

How Should We Pray?

We come now to the main part of this session, as we are, hopefully, by now convinced of the necessity of giving time to prayer. What then? The components of prayer may be summed up in the four attitudes mentioned in the previous paragraph: adoration, contrition, thanksgiving and supplication (easy to remember: ACTS). Let us deal with each one in turn.

ADORATION

This attitude of prayer can hardly be described in words. It is, in a sense, beyond words, and is experienced in silence. That saintly priest, the Curé of Ars, tells of an old man whom he saw, day after day, sitting on his own in the church. One day the priest went up to him and asked him what he was doing. 'Well,' said the man, 'I looks at him, and he looks at me – and we're both happy.'

That is the prayer of adoration, and silence is the key to it: a silence where the mind focuses, not on the past or the future, but on the present moment. A helpful means of this is to make use of some of the awareness exercises already described. For some, the use of a mantra can also be an aid. This consists of the mental repetition of a word or short phrase. Many people find a word in another language appropriate. In fact, this amounts to the repetition of a sound without any meaning attached, for example, the word 'Maranatha', which is the Greek for 'Come Lord', almost the last words of the New Testament (Revelation 22:20).

A shortened form of the Jesus prayer ('Lord Jesus Christ, Son of God, Saviour, have mercy on me, a sinner') is also often used – sometimes being shortened to just the name 'Jesus'.

Again, others will find they prefer a longer prayer: 'In You, O Lord, I place my trust', or 'The Lord is my light and my salvation'. Such repetition can lead to a depth of contemplation and adoration. As someone once said, 'It achieves a harmony of the disparate chords of life'. Try it and see!

I cannot emphasise enough, however, that adoration and contemplative prayer come about most of all through simple awareness – looking, listening, feeling, getting into the present moment.

CONTRITION

Continuing our classification of the different attitudes, or ends of prayer, we come to the importance of contrition. Jesus continually emphasises the importance of being reconciled with one another before turning to God in prayer (Matthew 5:23–24), and he put this into effect in a dramatic way as he hung, dying, on the cross: 'Father, forgive them; they do not know what they are doing.' And how many times do we repeat the phrase in the Lord's prayer, 'forgive us our sins *as we forgive* those who sin against us'? We can be sorry for our own sins, but forgiving others theirs is often difficult.

THANKSGIVING

St Paul tells us to be thankful in all circumstances (1 Thessalonians 5:16). So often we fail to be grateful for anything. To begin with there are the many different parts of our human body that function well: we forget this until a small part goes wrong!

So, we should be grateful for our sight, our hearing, the fact that we can walk or laugh or speak or sing and so on. Then there are the people around us: family, friends, colleagues, as well as the different happenings of each day. All that is straightforward. The difficulty comes when things go wrong. How can we be truly thankful then?

Firstly, there are our sins and failings. How can we thank and praise God for them? Yes, we can, *after* we have repented and turned back to God, because then he will draw good from them. Our Easter liturgy describes the sin of our first parents as a *felix culpa*, a happy fault, because through it a Saviour, the Son of God, became man. Secondly, after what is often necessary grief or anger at a particular happening, we should turn to God in our hearts and thank him for this. Then we are really trusting him and deepening our realisation that he is truly our loving Father. However, there are many occasions when we have to force ourselves to do this.

In his book *Sadhana*, Anthony de Mello tells the following story.

There is a Chinese story of an old farmer who had an old horse for tilling his fields. One day the horse escaped into the hills and when all the farmer's neighbours sympathised with the old man over his bad luck, the farmer replied, 'Bad luck? Good luck? Who knows?' A week later the horse returned with a herd of wild horses from the hills and this time the neighbours congratulated the farmer on his good luck.

His reply was, 'Good luck? Bad luck? Who knows?' Then, when the farmer's son was attempting to tame one of the wild horses, he fell off its back and broke his leg.

Everyone thought this very bad luck. Not the farmer, whose only reaction was, 'Bad luck? Good luck? Who knows?'

Some weeks later the army marched into the village and conscripted every able-bodied youth they found there.

When they saw the farmer's son with his broken leg they let him off.

Now was that good luck? bad luck? Who knows?

Father de Mello then adds:

Everything that seems on the surface to be an evil may be a good in disguise. And everything that seems good on the surface may really be an evil. So we are wise when we leave it to God to decide what is good luck and what bad, and thank him. Then we will share something of that marvellous mystical vision of Julian of Norwich who uttered what for me is the loveliest and most consoling sentence I have ever read: 'And all thing shall be well; and all thing shall be well; and all manner of thing shall be well!'

SUPPLICATION OR 'PETITION'

Most people, when they think of prayer, think immediately of the prayer of petition – asking God for this and that. Some, indeed, only pray when they want something. Petition is an important element in prayer, but, as we have tried to show, it is only part of it. Jesus spoke clearly of it (Matthew 7:7–11). He always answers our prayer, though not always in the way we are tempted to dictate to him. With our limited vision, we often cannot tell what is the best possible answer to our petition. This is illustrated by the story of the little girl who was travelling with her father on a fast train.

During the journey the little girl noticed the communication cord and her father explained to her how passengers could use it to have the train stopped. Some half an hour later she was standing by the open window, when suddenly the doll she had been holding fell out. In great distress she implored her father to pull the cord and stop the train. She cried, and without listening to his explanations, she went on: 'You can easily make it stop, Daddy, why don't you?' But he still refused.

Afterwards, in a calmer mood, she was able to understand that it would not be right to upset the timetable and put all the other travellers to inconvenience merely for the sake of a doll.

So it may be when God answers our petitions for temporal favours with a refusal. He likes us to ask for them, but he also likes us to leave the decision to him... Thy will be done, O Lord.

A few are tempted to give up praying because they think it is useless. After all, God does not change as a result of prayer. The response to that is that man, by means of prayer, makes himself attentive and receptive to the will of God, which, because the nature of God is perfect love, is always in our very best interests.

St Thomas says: 'We do not pray in order to change the divine determination, but to obtain that which God has determined should be brought about through prayer – that by asking, men may deserve to receive what almighty God has determined to give them from eternity'. We pray for temporal good in so far as it is not contrary to eternal good. It now remains for us to look, briefly, at a few of the many different ways of praying in our very rich Catholic tradition. Most of these ways consist of a blend of the four aspects we have been looking at.

THE DIVINE OFFICE OR BREVIARY

This is the official prayer of the Church. It comprises psalms, scripture readings, hymns and prayers and is arranged appropriately for the different times of the day – morning, midday, evening, night and so on. The psalms form an important part of this prayer of the Church, and whilst the sentiments expressed in them often fail to correspond to what we may be feeling at that particular moment, nevertheless, as they tell something of the gradual coming of God's Kingdom through the history of his chosen people, so we begin to realise that our own individual lives form a microcosm of this story, namely, the gradual opening up to God's love for each one of us.

THE ROSARY

Many people, not brought up as Catholics, find this form of prayer quite difficult. However, always remember the useful advice: 'Pray as you can, and not as you can't!' and if, after struggling, you are unable to be 'at home' with this prayer, don't worry – leave it! It may be that, later on, perhaps years later, you may find it more congenial.

With that proviso, let us now look at the rosary. It is in fact a kaleidoscope of prayer: meditation, mantra, praise, petition and so forth, and perhaps best compared to a song! As your fingers move over the beads, your lips, or mind, say the Our Father, the ten Hail Marys and the Glory be, and your thought is on one of the Joyful, Sorrowful or Glorious events in the life of Jesus, or, in the case of the last two, the glorious 'mysteries' (as they are called) of Our Lady. Some find it helpful to link the event in the life of Jesus with something happening in their own life for which they wish to pray, for example, in contemplating the birth of Jesus (the third joyful mystery), they will pray for the baby just born to a lady in the same street or the child they saw being baptised last week. With a little imagination you can link the events of two thousand years ago with events in the world today – Jesus continuing to live, suffer, die and rise again in our own lives.

Again, the rosary, as with all prayer, is like swimming: get into the water and try it out. A *Simple Prayer Book*, and most other prayer books, will give you the 'headings' for the various 'mysteries', and your sponsor will guide you in the use of the beads.

READING A PASSAGE FROM SCRIPTURE (DIVINA LECTIO)

To read a short passage, especially from one of the Gospels, imagining the whole setting, and that you are present there, taking part in it, and that, at some point, Jesus is turning to *you* and challenging you by his Word, or just by his Presence, can be a most fruitful way of praying. Most books on prayer explain this method very fully.

Always, what is most important is to find the best way of prayer for you at this particular point in your life; to give God the time; to persevere; and, finally, to be ready to change and modify how you spend that time according to the prompting of God's Holy Spirit, which is always there to lead us according to his way. So often, intellectually, our prayer doesn't need to make sense, as it is an outward expression of love. The little girl in the following story had the right idea.

An elderly gentleman passed his granddaughter's room one night and overheard her repeating the alphabet in an oddly reverent way.

'What on earth are you up to?' he asked.

'I'm saying my prayers,' explained the little girl. 'But I can't think of exactly the right words tonight, so I'm just saying all the letters. God will put them together for me, because he knows what I'm thinking.'

(Origin Unknown)

This is why praying 'in tongues' is a valid way of praying for those who have this gift. As St Paul says, '...the Spirit too comes to help us in our weakness, for, when we do not know how to pray properly, then the Spirit personally makes our petitions for us in groans that cannot be put into words...' (Romans 8:6) and, 'Those who speak in a tongue may build themselves up...' (1 Corinthians 14:4)

Remember: 'Pray as you can, and not as you can't!'

✝ *Prayer for this Session and During the Week*

It is usually good to begin the time of prayer with some of the awareness exercises suggested in session three.

Spend a few minutes thinking of something or someone for whom you wish to thank God.

Spend a few more minutes imagining someone for whom you wish to pray, sitting in front of you.

Imagine resting your hands on their shoulder or head and asking God to fill them with his love and peace and power.

? *For Discussion*

How do *you* pray?

What have you found helpful or unhelpful in this section on prayer?

What do you find easy and what do you find difficult about prayer?

Scripture Reading

Matthew 6:5–16

Also ponder on some of the texts already mentioned:
Luke 3:21; 4:1–13; 22:41–46 and so on.

For Further Reading

Sadhana by Anthony de Mello

Prayer by Abhishiktananda (SPCK) (Henri le Saux, OSB)

Prayers of Life by Michel Quoist (Gill & Macmillan)

Chapter Thirteen
The Sacraments in General: Signs of God's Love

The fundamental belief of our Catholic faith is that God loves us. He loves us, not because we are loveable, but simply because he is love (1 John 4:8). We do not earn his love. He doesn't love us more when we are good, or less when we sin. No, he loves us totally and completely, as if you or I were the only person who existed, and with an everlasting and unchanging love.

Peak Moments

As we become aware of this, we will want to express our poor response to this love, and the sacraments are the principal means (*not* the only means, of course) we have of doing this. They are the meeting points of God's love for us and our response to that love. We must not think of them as 'things' – one sometimes hears a parent say that they only want little Jimmy 'done', meaning baptised, or 'making' his first Holy Communion. These expressions are misleading. The sacraments are the high moments, peak moments in our relationship with God, through Jesus, and in the power, the love of the Holy Spirit. This is what we mean by 'grace'. They are the arms and hands of the Risen Christ living in and through his Church, which itself is the sacrament, the sign of Christ's Presence in the world.

God's Love

God shows his love for us in so many ways. He shows it through the beauty of creation; he has shown it in the history of his chosen people; it is seen whenever there is an act of unselfish love between two people; and he has shown it most of all by becoming one of us in Jesus. Jesus is love incarnate, love made flesh, tangible and manifest. Because we are human, most of us with sight and hearing and the sense of touch, we need to operate through these senses. Thus it is that Jesus continues to become love incarnate in the world today – through you and me, and, in a special way, through the sacraments.

Signs

The sacraments are different aspects of the presence of Jesus in our world and in our lives. They are the signs, that we can see, touch and understand, of the love of Christ for us.

If you see two yellow painted lines on the edge of the road, you know that means that you can't park your car there. Or if you see a red traffic light, you know that means you have to wait until it is green before you can move. These are signs. The description of a cloud in the Bible was a sign that the presence of God was there. The sacraments, then, are all signs that mark the presence of Jesus and the power of his love in the important moments of our lives, as well as in our daily journey from birth to death.

There is baptism, which begins our journey in faith and is essential prior to the reception of the others; confirmation, which is a stage further in the journey and strengthens us in the power of God's love; the sacraments of marriage and holy order mark a way of life we have embarked upon; the sacrament of reconciliation (confession) and the Eucharist, which we receive regularly on our journey through life; and the sacrament of the sick, which highlights the presence of Jesus in the midst of illness or when we are near to death.

Three of the sacraments (baptism, confirmation and holy order) imprint on us a 'character'. This is permanent and indestructible, and this is the reason why we can only receive them once in a lifetime. However, it is not like a piece of paper being marked with a rubber stamp. It is better described as a 'quality' or 'talent'. For example, my father, who had a great gift for playing the piano, lost most of the use of his right hand in the First World War. He could no longer play the piano as he used to. However, he still had the talent to play, although he was unable to use that talent as before. The talent he had was permanent, but his use of it was impeded by the accident.

Grace

All the sacraments involve, in some way or another, the 'laying on of hands', that is, the celebrant extends his hands over the person (or, in the case of the Eucharist, over the bread and wine). This is an ancient gesture indicating the 'pouring out' of God's grace and love and power. Intrinsically, of their very nature, all the sacraments convey the life and love of Christ, *but* the effectiveness of this depends on the spiritual state of the recipient. Throughout our lives we all need to grow in our openness to God and in our capacity to receive this power and new life God wants to give us, and which is infallibly present. Think about this.

A woman dreamt she walked into a brand new shop in the market place and, to her surprise, found God behind the counter.

'What do you sell here?' she asked.

'Everything your heart desires,' said God.

Hardly daring to believe what she was hearing, the woman decided to ask for the best things a human being could wish for. 'I want peace of mind and love and happiness and wisdom and freedom from fear,' she said. Then as an afterthought, she added, 'Not just for me. For everyone on earth.'

God smiled. 'I think you've got me wrong, my dear,' he said. 'We don't sell fruits here. Only seeds.'

This is why the Church demands at least a minimal response of faith before we receive any of the sacraments. They do not act automatically, like magic!

Some may recall that film of the life of St Vincent de Paul, in which Queen Anne of Austria engages in a dialogue with Vincent de Paul. The queen, turning towards St Vincent de Paul, says to him: 'You're doing too much, Monsieur Vincent.'

Vincent replied, 'I've done so little.'

The queen: 'You know you've done a great deal, and there will be few at judgement day who can give an account of days so well filled as yours.'

Vincent (with a gesture of despair): 'I have been idle, so terribly idle, ma'am; I have often been slothful.'

The queen said: 'Ah, Monsieur Vincent, we have thought of nothing but pleasure, of our appetite for enjoyment; and but for you these eyes of ours would never have been opened. Tell me, you who have thought of nothing but giving, you who have renounced happiness and power for ever, you who have built better things than vain palaces and idle renown, do you too, on the threshold of death, feel this great emptiness behind you?'

Vincent: 'Yes, ma'am, I have done nothing.'

The queen: 'What do you have to do, then, in one short life, if you are going to do something?'

And Vincent replied with this one word: 'MORE.'

Sacramentals

We have seen how special things, events and moments are hallowed, through the sacraments, as meeting points of God's love and ours. To help us grow in love and to remind us that all creation is God's, the Church, through her ministers, prays that certain objects, places and so on,

may always be used for a good purpose. The object (or it may be a person) is then said to be blessed. Such blessings are known as 'sacramentals', but they are not to be confused with the seven sacraments that we are now about to consider.

♰ *Prayers for this Session and During the Week*

LITANY OF HUMILITY

Cardinal Merry del Val was accustomed to recite the Litany of humility after the celebration of the Holy Mass. (To be 'filled with Christ', we must be empty of self.)

O Jesus! meek and humble of heart, Hear me

From the desire of being esteemed, Deliver me Jesus
From the desire of being loved,
From the desire of being extolled,
From the desire of being honoured,
From the desire of being praised,
From the desire of being preferred to others,
From the desire of being consulted,
From the desire of being approved,
From the fear of being humiliated,
From the fear of being despised,
From the fear of suffering rebukes,
From the fear of being calumniated,
From the fear of being forgotten,
From the fear of being ridiculed,
From the fear of being wronged,
From the fear of being suspected,

That others may be loved more than I, Jesus grant me the grace to desire it

That others may be esteemed more than I,
That in the opinion of the world
others may increase and I may decrease,
That others may be chosen and I set aside,

That others may be praised and I unnoticed,
That others may be preferred
to me in everything,
That others become holier than I,
provided that I may become as holy as I should.

? For Discussion

What other ways does God act in our lives, apart from through the sacraments?

🕮 Scripture Reading

1 John 4:7–12

🕮 For Further Reading

Healing through the Sacraments by Michael Marsch (Liturgical Press, Collegeville, USA)

Chapter Fourteen

The Sacraments of Baptism and Confirmation

The last instruction of Jesus before he 'disappeared from their sight' after the Resurrection, was, 'Go, therefore, make disciples of all nations; baptise them in the name of the Father and of the Son and of the Holy Spirit...' (Matthew 28:19)

Baptism precedes all the other sacraments. It is the first of what are known as the sacraments of initiation (baptism, confirmation and Eucharist). However, it is more than just an initiation ceremony, as when someone joins a club or society. It is more even than being caught up, belonging to the Christian community, the Church. It is a key moment of the 'journey in faith': the beginning of a life whereby we try to live out, day by day, the death and Resurrection of Jesus. We link the sufferings and joys with just these events in the life, death and risen life of Jesus, so that it is no longer we who live, but Jesus who lives in us.

Outward Sign of Baptism

This is one reason why the outward sign used in baptism is water, since water is a sign of death (you can drown in it), but it is also a sign of life (none of us could live without it). Ideally baptism should be by immersion – as it is done in the Baptist Church and recommended in the Catholic Church – whereby the person is, for a moment, totally immersed in the water, and then rises a new person to be clad in a new white garment. We can also see in water an ideal sign of what happens at baptism by remembering that it expands with both heat and cold: the baptised person, by praising God in all circumstances, both good and bad, also expands and becomes fulfilled and happy and at peace. Water is the source of life: all life came from the primeval waters, and we ourselves were born out of the water of the womb. All this is mentioned in the prayer of blessing of the water of the font at the Easter Vigil, when mention is made of the flight of the Israelites from Egypt which is seen as a 'figure' or foretaste of the Christian's journey through the waters of baptism.

Original Sin and Evil

We hear a great deal today about the pollution of our environment from fumes, dust and suchlike. We might also say that we live in a sin-polluted atmosphere, an atmosphere infested with evil. Evil is not just the absence of God, but the negation of God. It is a force, a power. We call it the devil. C.S. Lewis once said, 'Men don't believe in the devil now, as their fathers used to do; but what I'd like to know is who does the work the devil used to do?' God is love, and love involves freedom. Without freedom there can be no love, but with freedom there is always the possibility of the denial of love. Mgr. Ronald Knox puts it in this way:

> If God, in his great wisdom, was minded to create a universe in which our kind of moral goodness could operate, it must contain the possibility of evil. Not necessarily the actuality of evil; in theory, God might have been worshipped to all eternity by a world of angels and men that was capable of sinning, yet sinless. What happened – of course, I am talking in very crude terms and cutting all the corners – was that God created the possibility of evil and we actualised it.
>
> (Sermon preached at St Ethelreda's, Ely Place, 16th November 1952)

Baptism frees us from the effects of this sin-pollution. This is what we mean by original sin. God's love and power is always strong enough to protect us from it, provided we realise our dependence on God. Another way of looking at it is to think of someone being born in gaol. Baptism is rather like hauling them out of prison to a life of freedom. However, there is still the temptation to sin, and the possibility of falling again into sin – and this is why we have a third, and fourth, and fifth... an infinite number of second chances, provided we repent. We shall see this when we look at the renewal of our baptism in the sacrament of reconciliation (confession).

Infant Baptism

The general custom in the early Church was to wait until you were adult before being baptised. You would then answer for the faith you had grown to believe in and wished to practise. However, Christian parents, probably influenced by Jesus's own words, 'let the little children come to me', gradually expressed the wish for their babies to be baptised. In the case of adults, godparents were people who stood as guarantors that the person was indeed ready for baptism, but when it came to children being baptised, they took to answering for the faith of the child. In recent years the more realistic approach, in the case of infant baptism, is for the parents to answer for their own faith and their commitment to do their best to pass this knowledge and love of Christ on to their child.

Perhaps the main role of the godparents is that of prayer: to support the parents and the child by continued prayer for them.

At least one godparent should be a practising Catholic. The child (or adult) should, if possible, have at least one truly Christian name, the name of a saint, but beware of deaf clerics!

A Church of England vicar who was deaf asked the parents in the course of the baptism of their child, 'What name have you given your child?'

'Lucy, sir,' was the reply.

'Lucifer, Lucifer,' said the vicar. 'You can't give the child the name of the devil – I shall baptise him John!'

Belonging to the Church

Belonging as a full member of the Church involves baptism. However, there are degrees of membership of the Church, as we have seen already (Vatican II document on 'The Church', chapter two). A catechumen, as some of you may be, is someone who has not been baptised in any Church, but who is journeying towards baptism. Such a one has what we call 'baptism of desire'. The martyrs, who gave their lives for Christ, were conformed to their Saviour by the baptism of blood.

The Sacrament of Confirmation

If we receive the gift of God's life and love, the gift of the Holy Spirit, in the sacrament of baptism, we may well ask, 'What, then, is confirmation?' It is simply a new experience of the Holy Spirit, a further indwelling of that same Spirit we receive in baptism. The Apostles received this gift of the Spirit in the course of the Jewish feast of Pentecost (meaning fifty days after the Passover). It was a feast at which many pilgrims congregated in Jerusalem from all over the known world (Acts 2:5–13). At Jesus's baptism, three years previously, the Spirit is described as a dove, but at Pentecost it appears as fire and wind. These are all inadequate comparisons. How can one describe the power of God's love, a power that changed radically the recipients from being timid and afraid to being full of courage and confidence in the face of opposition?

In the first few chapters of Acts the word 'power' is used over forty times to describe the workings of the Holy Spirit. In Greek, the word used is *dunamis*, from which comes our word 'dynamite'. Pope John XXIII once told us: 'Go away, and make love grow everywhere.' All are called to do just this through whatever calling or vocation it may be – through marriage, through the single state, through the religious life, or through the priesthood or diaconate.

Signs

The dove underlines the 'brooding' and creative aspect of the Holy Spirit. Love is creative. God's love for us creates, and recreates us, and gives us a deep inner peace. Wind has always been a sign of the power of God. It can purify and at the same time blow a yacht to its destination. It is invisible but we see its effects. It causes great waves on the sea, and in a similar way arouses us from our lassitude. Like a draught, there is *no* place where it cannot enter.

Fire, like wind, purifies, but more completely. It gives light. It is the sign of the warmth of love of which Jesus spoke (Luke 12:49). It transforms all into itself, and spreads. For the Jews, fire was the sign of God's presence (Moses experienced God's presence in the burning bush).

The Spirit in Us

We see, then, how baptism gives us the gift of the Spirit and links us especially with the death and Resurrection of Jesus, the Easter event, whereas confirmation gives us a further gift of the Spirit, linking us with the coming of the Holy Spirit on the Apostles and their being sent off to spread the Good News far and wide, on the occasion of Pentecost. In other words, it helped them – and it applies to us, too – to live out the death and Resurrection of Jesus, to live out their baptism, and to bear witness to this by their lives and by their preaching.

Each one is called in a different way, and sometimes in unexpected and surprising ways, which means that we have to be prepared to accept and learn to appreciate one another. The following story illustrates this.

A family of five were enjoying a day at the beach. The children were bathing in the ocean and making castles in the sand, when in the distance a little old lady appeared. Her grey hair was blowing in the wind, and her clothes were dirty and ragged. She was muttering something to herself as she picked up things from the beach and put them in a bag.

The parents called the children to their side and told them to stay away from the old lady. As she passed by, bending down every now and then to pick things up, she smiled at the family. But her greeting wasn't returned.

Many weeks later they learnt that the little old lady had made it her lifelong crusade to pick up bits of glass from the beach so children wouldn't cut their feet.

(Father de Mello)

Through our baptism and confirmation, we may feel 'called' by the Lord to follow him as a single, celibate person, living alone or with others (for example, committed to a religious community dedicated to the service of the poor, nursing, teaching, social work); or as a married person, with the possibility of bringing up a family; or, again, as a priest given to proclaiming God's word in a diocese under the bishop, or belonging to a religious order.

In 1980, not long before he was assassinated, Archbishop Oscar Romero said:

> I repeat what I told you once before when we feared we might be left without a radio station: God's best microphone is Christ, and Christ's best microphone is the Church, and the Church is all of you. Let each one of you, in your own job, in your own vocation – nun, married person, bishop, priest, high school or university student, workman, labourer, market woman – each one in your own place live the faith intensely and feel that in your surroundings you are a true microphone of God our Lord.

✠ *Prayers for this Session and During the Week*

PRAYER OF ST FRANCIS OF ASSISI

Lord, make me an instrument of Thy Peace.
Where there is hatred, let me sow love;
where there is injury, pardon;
where there is darkness, light;
where there is sadness, joy.
O Divine Master,
grant that I may not so much seek
to be consoled, as to console;

to be understood, as to understand;
to be loved, as to love.
For it is in giving that we receive,
it is in pardoning that we are pardoned;
it is in dying that we are born to eternal life.

PRAYER TO THE HOLY SPIRIT

Come, O Holy Spirit, fill the hearts of your faithful,
and enkindle in them the fire of your love.
Send forth your Spirit and they shall be created.
And you shall renew the face of the earth.
Let us pray.
O God, who taught the hearts of the faithful by the light of the Holy Spirit, grant that by the gift of the same Spirit we may be always truly wise and ever rejoice in His consolation. Through Christ our Lord. Amen.

? *For Discussion*

How do you think you can be 'a true microphone of God'? (see quote by Archbishop Romero)

How have you dealt with evil in your life?

Scripture Reading

Acts 2:1–13

For Further Reading

Christianity Rediscovered by Vincent J. Donovan (SCM Press)

Chapter Fifteen
The Sacrament of Holy Orders

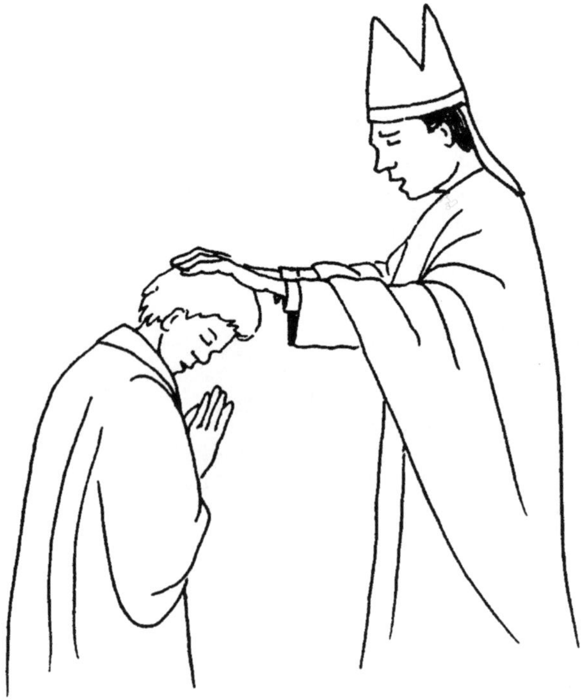

The Common Priesthood

We all share in the common priesthood of God's people through our baptism and confirmation. This means that all the baptised are called to offer themselves to God through Jesus Christ, the one High Priest. Similarly, all baptised are called to reflect in their lives some aspect of the life and ministry of Christ himself. It may take the form of being involved in some church activity or service – visiting the sick, comforting the bereaved, exercising the role of reader, Eucharistic minister, teacher or catechist, or, as we saw in the last session, living out our faith in whatever work we are engaged in.

The Ministerial Priesthood

Some, however, are called to serve Christ in what is called the ministerial or hierarchical priesthood, as deacons, presbyters (this is the correct term used by Vatican II, although the more general word 'priest' is still the more usual), or bishops. This is essentially different from the general and shared priesthood of all God's people. Jesus, at the Last Supper, commissioned his Apostles (and their successors, the bishops) to 'do this in remembrance of me.' (Luke 22:19) Thus, the fullness of this ministerial priesthood is to be found in the bishop, the direct successor, through the laying-on of hands, to the Apostles. The presbyter (or priest) and deacon share in it to a lesser degree, as helpers of the bishop.

All three are called to be ministers of the Word and means of sanctification for the people of God. This latter is the real meaning of the word 'hierarchy', which only later came to suggest 'rank'. The role of the deacon highlights the task of service in this ministerial priesthood of the Church.

Shepherds and Fishermen

The bishop, on certain official occasions, makes use of a crozier. This is often an ornate form of shepherd's crook, and reminds us of his role as shepherd. Jesus described himself as the good shepherd (John 10:11), passing on this task to his Apostles. He also told them to be like fishermen: 'Come after me and I will make you into fishers of people.' (Mark 1:18)

These really show the two aspects of the role of a bishop, and, indeed, of the Church as a whole, that is to say, to look after the sheep, the maintenance of the Church, but also to go out and catch more fish in the net, the missionary dimension of the Church. Both are necessary.

The Priest

At this stage, we might ask then, what is a priest (or presbyter)? He is not just the person who celebrates Mass and administers some of the other sacraments. Nor is he a one-man band doing everything in the Church. He is more like the conductor of an orchestra, drawing out the talents in each player. He is the leader and animator of a designated group of God's people, termed the parish. As participating in the bishop's role as 'minister of the Word', he must preach that Word by his life and actions and words, at all times, and in this way, be a reminder to all of God's love for them. His central task in this is the celebration of the Eucharist, at which he presides; in the name of all, and with all, he enables God's love to be made manifest and, at the same time, expresses our return of love to God, the Father. In a small Austrian village in 1945, Father Michael Richards recounts that a British soldier discovered that the local Catholic parish priest was called, not the rector, or the priest, nor vicar, father or clergyman, but *der geistlicher*, the man of the spirit. How good it would be if this were the manner in which all priests, deacons and bishops could be described.

The Call

The calling to the priesthood is not a direct phone call from God; it has to be discerned by the bishop and his advisors. Has the person seeking to follow training as a priest, or deacon, a generous nature? Does he mind a work that pays little and demands much? Is he interested in people – ready to listen and understand? Has he a spirit of obedience and a passion for sharing the love of God with others? One of our bishops, writing some years ago about vocations to the priesthood, stressed the importance of prayer in the family and of attitudes with regard to money and ambition shown within the family. Is prayer really important, and is money frittered away on unnecessary luxuries and pleasures? The call is always there, but the response is often lacking. The seeds are sown, but often fail to germinate, and discernment is necessary to discover the exact nature of the vocation to which a person is being called. It may be the priesthood, it may be the permanent diaconate, or it may be to live out in a more committed way the general priesthood of Christ brought about by baptism and confirmation. Only prayer and patience can reveal this. We are each different, with a slightly different calling. We must beware of being like the monkey who lifted a fish out of the water and placed it on the branch of a tree.

'What are you doing?' said another monkey.

'I'm saving it from drowning,' was the reply.

Celibacy

The discipline of celibacy in the Church has varied according to time and place. Most of the Apostles were probably married (Matthew 8:14 refers to Peter's mother-in-law). Jews regarded the blessing mentioned in Genesis 1:28 ('Increase and multiply...') as a divine command. Jesus, therefore, must have seemed completely out of order when he said that there were eunuchs for the sake of the Kingdom (Matthew 19:10–12). In some parts of the Catholic Church (for example, the Maronites) there has always been the option of marriage or celibacy (although ordination can only come subsequent to marriage, and not the other way round). The discipline (and it is not the dogmatic teaching) of the Church can, of course, continue to change in this matter. Suffice to say that there must always be in the Church at least some who follow Christ as celibates, as a sign and witness to the coming of the Kingdom, where there will be no giving in marriage, as we know it today. This can be hard, but then a good loving relationship in marriage will also involve the cross, and one is reminded of the words of Longfellow in the poem 'The Light of Stars'.

> Oh, fear not in a world like this,
> and thou shalt know ere long,
> know how sublime a thing it is
> to suffer and be strong.

The Cross

Perhaps the greatest heresy of our day is to try, at all costs, to avoid suffering, to avoid the cross, and to take what appears to be the easy way out. Fortunately, this is not the attitude of many young people, who are prepared to take up the challenge. Brother Roger Schutz of Taizé, who has experience of meeting so many thousands of young people each year, writes, 'I would go to the ends of the earth to speak over and over again of my confidence in the new generations, my confidence in the young. We who are older have to listen, and not condemn. They are blazing trails, overturning barriers, they will take the whole people of God with them.'

Canon Drinkwater tells the story of a listener to a radio programme who was disturbed, some years ago, by the celibacy of the clergy.

'You priests and your celibacy,' he said to a priest bitterly, 'tell me, have you yourself ever made anybody happy in your life?'

'Well,' replied the priest thoughtfully, 'you should at least agree I have made at least one person happier – the girl I didn't marry!'

Prayer for this Session and During the Week

Father

Pour out your Spirit
upon the people of our diocese,
and grant us
– a new vision of your glory,
– a new experience of your power,
– a new faithfulness to your Word,
– and a new consecration to your service,
so that your love may grow among us.
Show us the way ahead,
so that your kingdom may come,
through Christ Our Lord

Amen.

? *For Discussion*

Do you think all are called in some way or another? How?
How can the Christian faith help to answer that call?
What is the role of single people in the parish?

Scripture Reading

John 10:1–21

For Further Reading

A People of Priests: the Ministry of the Catholic Church by Michael Richards (DLT)

Chapter Sixteen
The Sacrament of Marriage

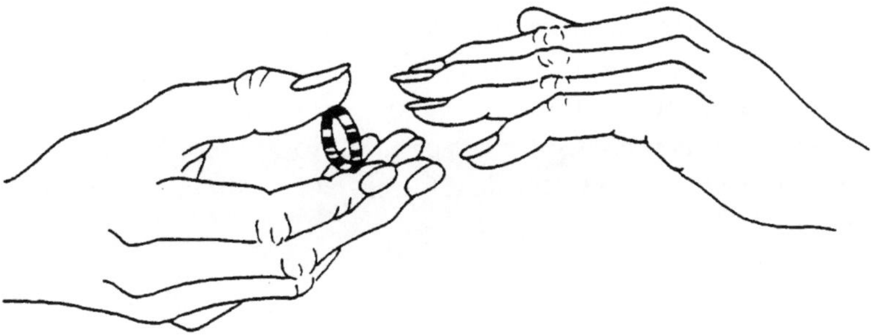

At the Time of Jesus

The backcloth to Jesus's teaching about marriage, and the Church's application of it, is not in some respects unlike the situation today. There was, at the time, an almost complete breakdown and collapse of marriage. In the Greek world, wives practised moral purity, living in total seclusion whilst their husbands exercised complete immoral licence. The temple priestesses in Corinth, for example, would walk the streets each evening. For the Romans, divorce was as common as marriage and there were women who numbered the years by the names of their husbands.

The Jews, however, upheld family life, and, in principle, divorce was not allowed. However a woman was very much regarded as 'a thing', with no legal rights. She was the possession of her father or her husband. There were two schools of thought amongst the Jews: some thought that a wife could be divorced if she committed fornication, whilst others claimed it was possible even if she only let her hair fall down or ruined the dinner!

Matthew, inbred as he was with his Jewish upbringing, has Jesus saying that divorce is possible for the reason of fornication. However, similar passages in the Gospels of Mark and Luke make no mention of this and merely uphold the very high ideal of marriage, as an unbroken union which, against the background of the world at that time, must have seemed even more difficult to uphold. However, it is this which the Catholic Church has taught consistently through the ages.

Love

We have begun this section on a slightly negative note, so let us now continue with a look at Jesus's overall teaching. This concerns the different aspects of love, and the seven sacraments, in particular, are the meeting points of love: the love of God for us, coupled with our poor, but nevertheless important, response to that love. Unfortunately, today when we use the word 'love', it is often unclear in what sense it is being used. In English we have only one word for what in Greek is expressed by four different words! There are, for example, different words for:

a) Family love (*Storge*): the love of parent for child or child for parent and so on.
b) Sexual love (*Eros*): the passion of a young man for a girl and vice versa.

c) Affectionate love (*Philia*): warm, tender affection, the highest kind of love.
d) Invincible goodwill, love (*Agape*): this means that no matter what a person does to us, we wish him or her well, and the highest good: it is a question of the will, and not of the feelings.

Perhaps we can now appreciate that the love of husband and wife embodies to some extent all four types of love, but mostly, of course, (b) and (c). With this in mind then, we can say that marriage is a sacrament, a sign of love, the giving of love from husband to wife and wife to husband. Jesus, by being present at a wedding feast and there performing his first miracle of changing water into wine, linked marriage with the Eucharist itself. This, as we shall soon see, is the abiding presence of his love and of his giving himself for us and to us (John 2:1–12). The Vatican II document on the Church in the modern world describes the meaning of love in marriage in this way:

> Man and woman, who by the marriage bond are 'no longer two but one' (Matthew 19:6) help and support each other in an intimate union of their personal beings and actions. Day by day they experience the meaning of their oneness and achieve it more fully. This mutual self-giving as well as the good of the children call for complete faithfulness and a union that is unbreakable.
>
> Christ blessed this love which springs from God and is like his union with the Church. Just as God encountered his people in a covenant of love and faithfulness (Ezekiel 16) so now Christ comes into the lives of married Christians through the sacrament of marriage. He remains with them, so that just as he loved the Church and gave himself up for her, the

married partners by their mutual gift may love each other with lasting faithfulness.

A Vocation

Marriage, then, is not just an administrative formality. It is the meeting of two loves: the love of a man and a woman with the love of Christ, caught up in the love that is of the nature of God himself. It is a 'community of love', an 'intimate partnership of love'. As such it is a vocation, a calling by God, a permanent and indissoluble union between man and woman, both a contract and, when between two baptised people, a sacrament.

Sacrificial

Furthermore, it is an ongoing sacrament. It is not limited to what happens in the church on the wedding day! The sacrament of marriage happens each day of married life. The romantic idea of falling in love and living happily ever after omits an important and vital element in the process of loving. In some sense or other, love in marriage always involves suffering and the cross. Love in marriage is a decision which has to be renewed daily, and this means a dying to self and one's own self-interest in order to give love and happiness to one's partner. This is perhaps best illustrated by the following story.

Two young people were very much in love and were hoping to get married. However, they were very poor, and when Christmas came, had no money for presents. So, without telling each other, each one decided to sell their most valued possession. The girl went to the hairdresser and had her beautiful long blond hair cut off. She then sold it and bought her fiancé a chain for his watch. Meanwhile, the young man went to the jeweller's and sold his watch in order to buy the girl two carved combs for her hair. They then exchanged their gifts, which proved to be a moment of tears followed by laughter. There was no watch for the chain, and no hair for the combs! However, there was something far more precious, and that was their unselfish and self-sacrificing love for each other.

(Origin Unknown)

Before Marriage

Many young couples today live together prior to marrying. Perhaps there can be cases where this does not involve premarital intercourse, which is the somewhat high-sounding expression for what Jesus called fornication. However, in most cases this is not so. The teaching of the Church, echoing Jesus's own teaching, is consistently opposed to 'sex before marriage', or fornication. It so often involves a selfish and greedy attitude: 'I must have that *now*.' It also involves fear – fear of losing the partner; and fear is opposed to love. Furthermore, there is always, to some extent, the fear of pregnancy, as no artificial form of contraception is infallible. The only completely safe form is to say 'No!' In other words, sexual union must only take place in the context of the permanent and binding union of marriage. There are, of course, some couples who live together with the understanding that their union is lifelong and permanent, but who do not wish for the hassle and expense of what they feel would be an elaborate church wedding. This is a pity, and the assumption behind it is false. Several of the best weddings I, as a priest, have witnessed (because the couple administer the sacrament to each other), have been without any of the 'frills', and with just the immediate family present.

Unitive and Procreative

The Church describes this bond in marriage which unites husband and wife as being both unitive and procreative. This means it tends to the oneness of the human couple *and* to the procreation of children. Now, if you think about it carefully, you will realise that all human acts in general comprise these two aspects – unitive and generative. To perform one action is to prepare the way for another; for example, the practice of surgery, learning a trade or skill, visiting a sick person. If, however, I block the act in some way, it is no longer a complete act of love. For example, if I say, 'I will give this money to this well-deserving missionary cause, but this is the last time I will do it,' then the act itself is harmed, and it is not an act of complete love. Contraception similarly damages the act itself. It is falling short of the total expression of love. This is equally true if we fail to do all we can to share our goods with other members of the human family who are in need.

Being Engaged

Preparation for the sacrament of marriage, especially in view of the current high divorce rate, is regarded as being of great importance, and most parishes have trained lay people involved in helping engaged couples prepare. Unfortunately, today many look first of all at the preparations for the wedding day, as opposed to preparing for the marriage itself. This latter involves giving time to think and talk together about their expectations, their attitudes regarding children, finance, communicating their feelings, their faith and so on. Good communication in a couple is a good means of growth in love. It has been said that 'to fail to prepare is to prepare to fail...'

A Valid Marriage

Something needs to be noted at this juncture concerning the Church's present discipline regarding who can be married in church and what constitutes the validity of a marriage, as confusion is rampant on these matters!

The first essential condition is for both parties to be free to marry (that is, not having been through a previous marriage which has not been annulled). Marriage between two non-Catholics in either a non-Catholic church or registry office is considered valid, but for the marriage of a Catholic with another Catholic, or with a non-Catholic, to be valid, it must be in a Catholic church or, with permission from the bishop, in a non-Catholic church. This is the basic principle of the Church's marriage discipline. If it can be shown that either party is not free to marry, or is being forced into marriage, for example, because of a pregnancy, or because they are insufficiently mature to make a lifelong commitment, then it is possible that there could be grounds for declaring the marriage null and void. The case would then have to be carefully examined by the Church's marriage tribunal. In the case of a Catholic marrying outside the Church (without the necessary permission), the marriage can be validated by a quite simple process, and this then enables the Catholic party or parties once again to receive the sacraments (reconciliation, Eucharist and so on) from which they would otherwise be barred.

It should be noted that, in danger of death, a Catholic who has previously been excluded from the sacramental life of the Church, may receive all the sacraments he or she may need.

Indissoluble

For a Christian there is no such thing as a trial marriage – 'If it doesn't work, then we can split up!' Marriage is, given its initial validity, indissoluble. This means that one important aspect of the life commitment is fidelity. In our modern culture and way of life, men and women mix together, at work or during recreation, far more than ever before. The temptations of infidelity are more common, and it is easy for a married man or woman to meet someone else of the opposite sex whom they find more sympathetic and easier to get on with in some ways than their partner. Perhaps they are going through a difficult patch at home, and then, before they know where they are, they realise they are 'in love' with another person!

Each day one has to say, 'I have committed myself to my partner, for better for worse. In this love and this commitment I will find the cross, but I must, with the strength and power of God, steer through this cross and, through it, find new life in Jesus.'

A Happy Marriage

One might, then, be tempted to ask the question: 'Is happiness in married life possible? Is complete harmony between a couple possible?' The answer is 'no', if the proof of many modern films, books and plays is anything to go by. However, the answer is a definite 'yes', if we look at the joy and contentment in so many homes around us. Usually, these fail to hit the front-page news!

The total commitment in marriage must be based on trust – a trust which, hopefully, grows over the years, and involves the acceptance of one's partner with all their faults and failings, as well as their good qualities. We so often want to change the person we love into the ideal, but this can never be. Acceptance of the other as they are is essential (of course, if one sees one's partner behaving immorally, for example, stealing money from work, then one has an obligation, gently and kindly, to correct), without trying to 'take them over', to control them or overwhelm them, so that they lose their freedom. Daily forgiveness of the little hiccups in the relationship, followed by reconciliation, can enable a really deep and lasting love to grow and develop, and nourished by a good sense of humour, it can solve many a problem or period of tension.

Renewal

The sacrament of marriage, then, administered by the couple to each other, is a sacrament of growth, and for this reason it is good, at stages in one's life, and indeed regularly, annually, to renew one's commitment. Both the expression and the quality of one's love changes and, hopefully, grows and develops. Some parishes give, each year, the opportunity for all married couples to renew their commitment. This sometimes happens on the Feast of the Holy Family, just after Christmas. Each promises to continue to love and cherish, to heal and sustain in the frequently difficult day-to-day living of family life. This can be particularly important at the time of the mid-life crisis, or when the last of the offspring has left the family nest.

Prayer Together

Where there is love, there is God; and an awareness of God's presence in marriage is important for a couple who share belief in God, and even more so for those who share the same Christian faith. This is where prayer comes in – prayer together, which may be just sitting side by side, hand in hand, and being still and quiet for a few minutes, each one communing with God in their own personal way. Couples who do this usually find that there comes a time when one or the other wants to share their thoughts, their thanks to God, or their prayer for someone they know... The saying goes that a family that prays together, stays together.

Being Caught Up in the Love That Is God

Finally, loving another in marriage means being caught up in God's love, which has been shown most clearly in the death and Resurrection of Jesus. Love always involves suffering, but it also always involves great inner joy and peace. It is the reverse of the case of the lady in the story recounted by Lionel Blue.

> Two women went for a safari holiday in Africa. As they were going through the bush a great gorilla leaped out at them.
>
> One of them managed to get away, but the gorilla grabbed the other and embraced her, and he took her back to his cave and embraced her again... and again... and again...
>
> A few days later a rescue party came and she was put in hospital suffering from shock. The other woman, who had made her way back to civilisation, visited her in hospital.
>
> She sat by her bed and asked, 'Well, how do you feel?'

Her friend replied, 'How should I feel? – he doesn't ring, he doesn't write.' She sighed.

'No grapes...'

☩ *Prayer for this Session and During the Week*

FOR RENEWAL OF MARRIAGE VOWS

O God, I thank you that you have given us another year of life together. I thank you for the love which grows more precious, and for the bonds which grow more close every day. I thank you for the happiness we have known together; for the experience of sunshine and of shadow through which we have come.

I ask your forgiveness for any disloyalty on my part; for any times when I was difficult to live with; for any selfishness and inconsiderateness; for any lack of sympathy which spoiled, even for a moment, the perfect relationship which marriage should be.

Spare us to each other to go on walking the way of life together, and grant that for us it may be true that the best is yet to be.

Through Jesus Christ Our Lord. Amen.

(William Barclay)

? *For Discussion*

What are your ideas on marriage?

Do you think Christian marriage is difficult?

Scripture Reading

Matthew 5:31–32; 19:3–9

John 2:1–2

1 John 4:7–17

For Further Reading

The Art of Loving by Erich Fromm (Unwin Books)

Chapter Seventeen
The Sacrament of Reconciliation

Healing

All the sacraments are to some extent sacraments of healing, but the next two we are to consider, the sacrament of reconciliation and the sacrament of the sick, show in a particular manner the healing power of Jesus.

The sacrament of reconciliation may be regarded as the means of being renewed in our baptismal state. It is a sacrament of restoration. The great Catholic poet, Francis Thompson, and countless others found this. Francis was a failed student, book agent, shoemaker's apprentice and soldier. He became a drug addict, until Wilfred Meynell, an editor, found him and gave him a home. Francis then wrote one of the greatest of English poems, 'The Hound of Heaven':

I fled him, down the nights and down the days;
I fled him down the arches of the years;
I fled him, down the labyrinthine ways of my own
  mind; and in the mist of tears
I hid from him...

In the introduction to the rite of this sacrament, St Ambrose is quoted: 'The Church possesses both water and tears; the water of baptism, the tears of penance.'

Sin

The sacrament we are looking at now, then, is a sacrament of mercy, of forgiveness. However, this presumes that there is sin to deal with. What, then, is sin? It is essentially a deliberate turning away from God, from what is recognised as good, and being 'secure' in ourselves! It is the setting up of oneself as being 'in charge'. 'I' is at the centre of 'sin'. In some cases this can be serious (sometimes called 'mortal sin', by which man turns away from God); but more often than not it is less serious ('venial', which retards a man in the pursuit of his end), and is often due to a partial blindness in our outlook (for example, the many good things we could do, but fail to do), or just a general failure to continue growing in God's way and being open to the inner prompting of God's love.

Jesus knew perfectly the way our human nature works. He experienced it himself. 'He was like us in all things, except sin.' However, he knew what temptation to sin was. Read Matthew's Gospel, 4:1–11 and 26:36–46 in Gethsemane. There must have been many other instances when he was tempted. He spoke frequently about sin, coupling it always with the importance of repentance and God's love and mercy.

The Prodigal Son

Jesus's story of 'The Prodigal Son' (sometimes described as the story of 'The Forgiving Father') sums up for us best of all his teaching on sin, repentance and forgiveness. Take time to read this slowly and carefully (Luke 15:11–32).

In the older son who stayed at home, we find:

- Pride

  He was number one. He considered himself the most important. He was secure in himself and in his position. All sin is linked with pride. The temptation of our first parents was 'to be as gods'. This was pride.

- Envy
  He was envious, jealous of his younger brother when he was specially favoured.
- Anger
  He ranted and raved at his father, and then sulked, refusing to go into the house. He felt his former obedience to his father had not been recognised. He was resentful and failed to forgive his brother as his father had done.

Then, in the younger son, the prodigal, we see:

- Avarice
  He was after the inheritance. He loved money to spend on himself.
- Gluttony
  One area of his spending was on food and drink, which he indulged in to excess. Our society today has been described as 'the great grub society organised around the business of eating...'
- Lust
  He indulged in his craving for sexual satisfaction – sex separated from the total love of another person.
- Sloth
  He had no wish to work for his living; no wish to try to bring happiness and joy into anyone's life; content only to be lazy and live off his inheritance.

The Father's Love

We see, however, that the younger son repented, but the older one continued in his separation from the household. The repentance of the younger son is welcomed by the father, who is open-armed, immediately offering complete forgiveness and mercy and love. And so we come back to the importance of realising God's love for us and trusting him. 'Do not be afraid...' This parable of Jesus's sets out so clearly God's love for us, and the different ways we can sin and turn away from that love. The seven attitudes or sins mentioned above are described by the Church as the seven capital sins.

How, then, did Jesus deal with this sin situation of ours? Firstly he proclaimed the forgiveness of sin, and it was precisely this that aggravated many of his hearers, for only God can forgive sin (Luke 5:21). But not only did he forgive sin, he went a step further and gave power to his Apostles to do the same. They, too, are to be ministers of forgiveness and reconciliation. 'As the father sent me, so am I sending you.' After saying this he breathed on them and said, 'Receive the Holy Spirit. If you forgive anyone's sins, they are forgiven; if you retain anyone's sins, they are retained.' (John 20:21–23)

The oldest law in the world is the *Lex Talionis* of Hammurabi which goes back some four thousand years. By this the punishment must not be greater than the injury: the principle of 'let the punishment fit the crime'. This, in its time, was a great step forward, as hitherto, if several cattle were stolen from one group of people, the guilty parties could be literally wiped out! Jesus, in his teaching on forgiveness, did away with the very principle of this law: retaliation has no place for the follower of Jesus. Love your enemies, forgive as we ask God to forgive us, and bear no resentment!

History of the Sacrament

We will now see, briefly, how this command of the Lord was carried out by Jesus's followers, and in doing this we will see how the seed sown by Jesus has grown, changed and developed in a number of ways over the centuries. As far as we can tell, in the first centuries, confession of sin was public, prior to the celebration of the Eucharist, and it concerned only three major sins – murder, adultery or fornication, and apostasy (going the way of the world and giving undue reverence to the Roman Emperor, who set himself up as God). After confession of one of these sins, the penitent would join with Christ's once-and-for-all atonement for sin by performing some kind of penance, and would then be reconciled with the Christian community by absolution. Moreover, you could only go to confession once in a lifetime. It was regarded as a 'second chance' subsequent to baptism. Unfortunately, legalism rapidly crept in whereby people postponed their baptism until their deathbed. After all, subsequent to baptism, there was only one more chance...

The Church had to await the spread of the influence of the Irish monks with St Columba in the sixth century for confession to become private, and for Jesus's words to Peter to become effective:

> Then Peter went up to him and said, 'Lord, how often must I forgive my brother if he wrongs me? As often as seven times?' Jesus answered, 'Not seven, I tell you, but seventy-seven times.'
>
> (Matthew 18:22)

There was to be no limit set to forgiveness! Furthermore, Jesus showed this in practice when from the cross he forgave his murderers (Luke 23:34).

From being private, confession of sins soon became absolutely secret, whereby nothing a penitent told the priest regarding his sins could be divulged or made use of; and this is how it has remained to this day. One disadvantage of this and also of the introduction of the confessional grille in the sixteenth century, was to underestimate the community nature of sin. All sin is against God, but all sin also affects other people. Even the most private of sins or failings affects others because it makes the sinner less of the being that God wants him to be, and so affects his relationship with others. All sin is then, to some extent, social.

In our own day, this is being emphasised more by the custom of 'Services of Reconciliation', whereby we prepare together for individual confession and absolution, or, in some special cases, a general and public absolution. This helps us realise that sin is a community failure, and the priest in confession is the sign of the all-forgiving Lord, extending his arms of love and mercy to us, but also of a forgiving and loving community to which we are reconciled.

One element in the confession of sin was the imposition of a 'penance' (prayer or good works), to be performed. This was an outward sign of being, as it were, joined to the complete and perfect satisfaction for sin shown by Jesus in his sacrifice on the cross. Later in the history of the sacrament these penances could be acquitted by the gaining of 'indulgences'. These are the remission, in whole or part, of the temporal punishment due to sin already forgiven. It had all become somewhat mathematical; but we must remember that the underlying idea was really the union of all of us in the Body of Christ: the saints can help us and we can help one another through our prayer and good works.

What to Confess

We will look at the practical details of how a Catholic actually 'goes to confession', later in the course of the Lenten period of preparation; and we shall see that some of the things seen on *The Dave Allen Show* are a gross parody of the reality! Remember that all Catholics trying to practise their faith and grow in the love of God and of one another go to confession regularly. The Pope does, so do the bishops, priests and laity. The closer we come to the Lord, the more we realise the gulf between God's goodness and our own sinfulness, our pride, our greed and our selfishness. Our small failings do matter: they are the nuts and bolts of our lives and of our love. Big sins develop from small ones.

Some years ago there was a plane crash in which twenty-seven people were killed. At first, many theories were put forward to explain why it had happened. Finally it was revealed that a small screw in the instrument panel had not been properly tightened when it was being made. In use, it had loosened a few more turns, with the result that the dial had been obstructed. The pilot made a miscalculation and the plane crashed... all due to the slight carelessness on the part of a worker in the factory... Little things do matter.

Before concluding this topic, we might ask the question, '*Why* confess my sins?' Certainly, if we are truly sorry in our hearts – and this is always, of course, essential – then God forgives us. However, we do need outward signs. We are incarnate, people of flesh and blood, and we express ourselves through word and gesture. God came down to this earthly level of ours and so it is necessary to meet him on this level as well as on the 'purely spiritual'. This is the reason for the sacraments, and that of reconciliation in particular. It is an outward sign of true repentance and a guarantee of God's forgiveness.

However, as in the story of 'The Prodigal Son' with which we began this session, the father's love and forgiveness is always paramount. His love transforms our sins so that we can say, *O felix culpa* (Oh, happy fault...). Think about the moral of this story:

A great artist, famous for painting hills and forests, rivers and wild places, stayed one holiday in a great house in the north of Scotland. The lady of the house was very proud of her home, and had had

some of it decorated just before inviting a number of guests to stay with her. But one of them, accidentally, broke a bottle he was carrying and splashed the contents across one of the newly decorated walls – a great ugly stain on the lovely new wallpaper.

The poor visitor felt awful, of course: and the hostess was very annoyed. But next day when all the rest of the party went hunting, the artist, Landseer, stayed indoors. And when he was alone he stared for a long time at that disfiguring mark on the wall. Then he took his charcoal and paints and began to work upon the wall. Soon the dark splash became a tumbling waterfall; above it a high hill, rocky crags, fir trees, and, gazing at it all, on the other side, a fine stag with great branched horns. Landseer had transformed that ugly stain into something very beautiful.

(Origin Unknown)

✞ *Prayer for this Session and During the Week*

Spend a few minutes on the awareness exercises. Then think of one thing that went wrong through your own fault in the recent past. Tell God, in your heart, how sorry you are for this. Pray for anyone who may have been hurt through it.

? *For Discussion*

What 'gods' are there in your life?
How would you feel about going to confession?

Scripture Reading

Matthew 4:1–11; 26:36–46, 18:18, 21–35
John 20:21–23
Luke 15:11–32

For Further Reading

The Screwtape Letters by C.S. Lewis (Collins)

Chapter Eighteen
The Sacrament of the Sick

Why Suffering?

There is a Peanuts cartoon which shows Charlie Brown lying down at night talking to the Lord. 'Lord,' he says, 'I have a question for you... Why am I sleeping in a cardboard box? Why do I always have to suffer like this? Why me, Lord...?' And then you see him going to sleep, and saying, 'Don't answer that, Lord!'

That, perhaps, aptly sums up our reaction to suffering... and there *is* no rational explanation of suffering. It is part of life: what is dead cannot suffer. It is a part of loving: love inevitably involves suffering. The reverse, however, does not necessarily follow – suffering may not lead to love. Similarly, sin, the failure to love, also leads to suffering, but it is not true to say, as did many of the Jews up to the time of Christ, that suffering implies sin (for example, John 9:1–13).

We believe in a God who is total goodness, perfect love, and so, inevitably, from time to time we continue to pose the question, 'Why does God allow suffering?' The most we can do is indicate a few pointers, realising, however, that ultimately we are faced with a mystery.

a) God does not want suffering. He doesn't enjoy it – like the boy who pulls the wings off the butterfly. We shall see shortly that Jesus spent much time alleviating suffering. However, he does sometimes allow it so that a greater good may result – like the pruning of a tree (John 15:1–17). Or as someone less elegantly expressed it, suffering is like manure, it is unpleasant and to be avoided, but growth comes through it. Similarly, when asked what he did for his disciples, the teacher said, 'What a sculptor does for the statue of a tiger: he takes a block of marble and pounds away at anything that doesn't look like a tiger.' When his disciples later asked exactly what he meant, the teacher said, 'My task is to hammer away at everything that isn't you; every thought, feeling, attitude, compulsion that adheres to you from your culture and your past.'
b) Much suffering is due to the misuse of our free will; for example, selfishness, greed, thoughtlessness. If I am an inquisitive person and put my eye to the keyhole to see what is happening in the room, and end up with a swollen eye, then this suffering is the direct result of my sin. We could only abolish this sort of suffering by being deprived of our freedom, and then we'd be 'action men', puppets, inhuman.

c) Suffering can be because we are trying to follow the way of Christ; for example, throughout the ages, Christians have been persecuted and sometimes martyred simply because they are Christian; others have suffered because they have refused to be caught up in immoral dealings at work.

d) Again, suffering can be self-inflicted in the form of penance. This is something like the pruning of the tree mentioned above. Lenten penance, or Friday penance, is voluntary, with the purpose of becoming more as the Lord wants us to be. Fasting and abstinence is, or should be, geared so that we have more time, energy and money to help those in need, as well as being a means of self-discipline.

e) Bereavement and separation are forms of suffering we all have to experience at some time or other, and they are real crosses which, although becoming less acute with time, never completely disappear.

f) Finally, there is the suffering of the innocent and that caused by natural disasters. These are the most difficult to accept, and impossible to understand or make sense of. We can but look at Jesus, the God-man, who was perfectly innocent and yet suffered appallingly. We can only shed a tiny glimpse of light on the mystery by reminding ourselves that this life is but a very brief preparation for the next, the fullness of life with God, and our suffering can become redemptive if joined with that of Jesus.

Furthermore, for the most part, God isn't going to be continually stepping into his creation and cutting across the laws that he himself has brought about. Sometimes, as a sign of his power and his love, he does, in a vivid way, step in; and always, if we turn to him, he brings good out of evil and suffering.

Healing

A non-Catholic once said that the most important lesson a person can learn from his life is not that there is pain and suffering in the world, but that it depends on us to turn it to good account. In the past there was a little too much emphasis on the redemptive value of suffering, and hardly any reference to the healing power of God through the sacraments and in other ways. Today the pendulum has swung the other way, and perhaps there is too much accent on healing to the exclusion of the redemptive nature of suffering. At all costs, people today want to eliminate pain completely; for example, in childbirth, at the dentist, after an operation, not to mention the terminally ill – the ever open aspirin bottle is symbolic of this. This attitude also affects human relationships: the slightest conflict or suffering in a marital relationship so easily leads to divorce. It is the attitude of 'The Great Escape from the Cross'.

C.S. Lewis writes that God whispers to us in our pleasures, speaks to us in our conscience, but shouts in our pains: it is his megaphone to rouse a deaf world! Having said that, let us now look at Jesus's attitude to the sick and suffering. Yes, he did want to heal – though not everyone was healed; but the greatest, perfect healing is always, for all of us, death – death which leads to resurrection and the glorification of our bodies, minds, wills and spirits. 'Healing is a step towards the cross, in that healing removes some of the obstacles to freely embracing the cross.'

Jesus showed God's love and wish for us to be healed and whole in different circumstances in his three year public ministry, and he commissioned his disciples to do likewise: 'So they set off to proclaim repentance; and they cast out many devils, and anointed many sick people with oil and cured them.' (Mark 6:12–13)

It was a Jewish custom, at the time of Jesus, to have a jar of perfumed oil just inside the door, and a guest coming to the house would have their tired and dusty feet washed and then anointed with the oil. An important visitor would be anointed on the hands and head as well. It was for this reason that royalty and bishops began to wear crowns and mitres so that the oil didn't get into their eyes! Oil is thus a sign of cleansing, comfort, strength and protection. Hence we are not surprised to find that already in the early Church the sick were anointed: 'Any one of you who is ill should send for the elders of the church, and they must anoint the sick person with oil in the name of the Lord, and pray over him. The prayer of faith will save the sick person and the Lord will raise him up again; and if he has committed any sins, he will be forgiven.' (James 5:14–15)

The Sacrament of Healing

Over the centuries, this anointing of the sick, as happened with the sacrament of baptism for a time, came to be linked with a deathbed repentance, known as 'Extreme Unction' or 'The Last Rites'. The use of these terms, unfortunately, still lingers on. There was a teacher who one day asked her class how many sacraments there were. A little girl put up her hand and said, 'None, Miss. My grandmother had the last yesterday!' In recent years the Church has emphasised that it is the sacrament of the sick and, as such, a sacrament of healing and of life. It is the very reverse of being the last. So often it results in renewed health in mind and body, and, through it, sin is forgiven and peace comes to the sick person.

The sacrament may be given to anyone who is seriously ill, or whose illness is likely to lead to some concern, anyone about to have a major operation, or an elderly person who has begun to 'feel the weight of years'. It may also be given at each successive stage of illness. Bishop Francis Thomas, who experienced the different stages of cancer over a period of a year, was anointed no less than seven times, and each time found great peace and comfort through the sacrament. It is, perhaps, the inner healing of mind and will and heart that is most important, but because we are one whole person, this can often have an effect on our bodies. It has been estimated that fifty per cent to eighty per cent of all diseases have their origins in emotional stress. In late adolescence we begin to accumulate the effects of stress that will surface as physical disorders in our forties and fifties.

It is quite common these days to hear of 'healing services'. They might be better described as 'services of blessing and prayer for the sick'. They do not necessarily include the sacrament of the sick, but may include the 'laying on of hands' or 'praying over' the sick. This can be a great help and a means of healing – mental, emotional and physical.

Using All Possible Means for Healing

God's healing power works through all possible means, and whereas the spiritual part of us is paramount, this sacrament of healing must be seen as the sign of God's love and healing power shown through the doctors and nurses and all who are caring for the sick person. Recent advances in surgery, for example, surely point to the marvels of God's creative and healing power.

In the days of Communist Russia, Douglas Woodruffe wrote in *The Tablet*:

> At an international gathering of surgeons there was discussion about what is the most delicate and difficult operation which confronts modern surgeons. An American said he thought operations of the heart, but his English colleague, a brain surgeon, argued that for the extreme precision required and the damage that could be done by the slightest variation he thought operations on the brain took pride of place. 'And I,' said the Russian colleague thoughtfully, 'find that the most delicate and difficult of all operations is the removal of tonsils.' 'The tonsils!' they exclaimed. 'Surely that is the simplest and commonest operation of all!' 'Ah,' said the Russian, 'but you must remember that in the Soviet Union, where everyone must keep his mouth shut, we surgeons have to work from the other end.'

Conclusion

On a more serious note, much of this section is summed up in the words of Viktor Frankl in his book, *Man's Search for Meaning*.

> Whenever one is confronted with an inescapable, unavoidable situation, whenever one had to face a fate which cannot be changed, for example, an incurable disease, such as inoperable cancer; just then one is given a last chance to actualise the highest value, to fulfil the deepest meaning, the meaning of suffering. For what matters above all is the attitude we take towards suffering, the attitude in which we take our suffering upon ourselves.
>
> Let me cite a clear-cut example. Once an elderly general practitioner consulted me because of his severe depression. He could not overcome the loss of his wife who had died two years before and whom he had loved above all else. Now how could I help him? What would I tell him? Well, I refrained from telling him anything but instead confronted him with the question, 'What would have happened, Doctor, if you had died first, and your wife had had to survive you?' 'Oh,' he said, 'for her this would have been terrible; how she would have suffered!' Whereupon I replied, 'You see Doctor, such a suffering has been spared her, and it was you who spared her this suffering; but now, you have to pay for it by surviving and mourning her.' He said no word but shook my hand and calmly left my office. Suffering ceases to be suffering in some way at the moment it finds a meaning, such as the meaning of a sacrifice.

The sacrament of the sick helps us, most of all, to draw nearer to the meaning of suffering by drawing us closer to Jesus, who suffered for us all.

✠ *Prayer for this Session and During the Week*

In Ravensbruck an unknown prisoner wrote this prayer on a torn piece of wrapping paper and left it on the body of a dead child.

Oh Lord, remember not only the men and women of good will, but also those of ill will. But do not remember all the suffering they have inflicted on us; remember the good effects we have brought thanks to this suffering – our comradeship, our loyalty, our humility, our courage, our generosity, the greatness of heart which has come out of this and when they come to judgement, let all the fruits we have borne be their forgiveness.

God, our Father, you sent your only Son, Jesus, on earth to heal a broken-hearted and wounded world. He had compassion on those who called on Him for help and healing. He touched the sick and guilt-laden, and they walked away in health and freedom of spirit. Visit us now with His saving power so that we too may be released in mind and body to praise your healing grace through Christ our Lord. Amen.

When the signs of age begin to mark my body (and still more, when they touch my mind); when the ill that is to diminish me or carry me off strikes from without or is born within me; when the painful moment comes in which I suddenly awaken to the fact that I am ill or growing old; and above all, at the last moment when I feel I am losing hold of myself and am absolutely passive within the hands of the greatest unknown forces that have formed me; in all those dark moments, O God, grant that I may understand that it is You (provided my faith is strong enough) who are painfully parting the fibres of my being, in order to penetrate to the very marrow of my substance and bear me away within Yourself...

(Teilhard de Chardin)

? *For Discussion*

How do you react to suffering, in yourself and in others?

🕮 *Scripture Reading*

Mark 16:14–18
James 5:12–17

🕮 *For Further Reading*

Man's Search for Meaning by Viktor Frankl
In the Hour of His Distress by Bishop Francis Thomas (Diocese of Northampton)

Chapter Nineteen
The Background to the Eucharist: The Passover

We come now to the most important sacrament of all, which is, in a sense, far more than a sacrament. For this reason we have left it until last. We looked at it somewhat superficially in the enquiry stage of our journey in faith, but now we must see how it originated in the earliest ages of mankind.

Primitive Man

Man has always wished to express his relationship with the power he believed to be controlling the forces of nature around him. This might have been inspired by fear, or by love, or, more often, by a combination of the two, but normally with fear uppermost. He expressed these feelings by giving a sort of 'cupboard love'.

If he was settled in one place, he would offer to the deity (whatever form this might take: wooden or stone idol and so on) the first fruits of his crop, considered the best; or if he was a nomad, a wanderer, he would give to the god the first-born animal of his herd, for example, a lamb. This would be killed, ceremoniously offered to the god or gods, consumed and the remains destroyed. The eating of what had been offered to the god(s), that had, in some mysterious way, had contact with the deity through the offering, would enable the offerer, if he consumed it, also to have contact with the god.

Covenant

This then developed into a 'covenant meal', which took on various forms. The full meaning of it was often seen in the nomadic herdsmen who were the forefathers of the Hebrew nation. They would make a 'covenant' with a neighbouring tribe by killing an animal, slicing its carcass in two and laying the two halves on the ground side by side. The parties to the contract would walk between the two halves, asking that the same fate might befall them if ever they broke their covenant.

For us a covenant is merely an agreement, a pact, a legal contract. But for the Jews and the people of the Middle East in general, it meant an alliance of a particularly intense and sacred kind. It created a kinship between men that was only one step removed from the holy ties of blood.

If a clan entered into a covenant with a neighbouring tribe, in effect, the two became one community, one people. In choosing each other, they were joined together so closely that they actually came to belong to each other. Both parties swore on oath to keep their mutual agreement and abide by it for ever. Once sworn, the oath was inviolable. Once the agreement had been spoken and the sacred 'Amen' uttered, then the conditions of the covenant were binding and could not be broken.

The blood that ran fresh and steaming from the newly slaughtered beast would often be collected in a receptacle and sprinkled over the two groups of people. This blood of the covenant was regarded as sacred:

- It signified death; breathing stopped, and breath was the 'life force' (on a cold day the breath was visible and blood steamed in the same way).
- Hence it was thought that the breath of life must reside in the blood stream.
- Hence blood, when freshly shed, and before the breath had left it, was regarded as liquid life.
- But life was holy. Therefore blood was holy. So it was used for purifying buildings, consecrating altars and sealing covenants.

The Hebrews embodied in their worship these ways of ratifying a covenant – killing a lamb, sprinkling the blood and eating a sacred meal – and developed it into what became the Passover meal. It became a sign of the covenant between the one God, Yahweh (I am who I am), and his chosen people, the Hebrews.

Passover

Now, later, when the Hebrews arrived in Palestine, they found the pagans there already celebrating a sort of springtime feast. The pagans made a clean sweep and a fresh start – they got rid of all their old bread and flour and yeast and they baked a fresh batch of bread from the first sheaf of the barley harvest. But there was no time to grow a new culture of yeast, so this bread had to remain unleavened.

And so the day came to be known as the feast of the unleavened bread. This feast was taken up by the Jews and included in their Passover celebrations. The unleavened loaves also reminded them of the haste with which their ancestors had fled from Egypt, with no time to put in the yeast!

By the time of Jesus, the Passover feast, celebrating the escape from Egypt, followed a well-established pattern. Some 250,000 lambs were offered to God and slaughtered in the temple in Jerusalem. Each family would take sufficient home to be prepared and cooked. This would be combined with various other ingredients reminding them of the bitterness of their slavery in Egypt, their hasty escape, and their miraculous passing to safety through the waters of the Sea of Reeds. The blood, of course, was completely drained from the meat before it was taken from the temple, owing to the aforementioned belief about the sacredness of blood (hence Jewish kosher food).

The Lamb of God

Jesus embodied in himself the whole of this long history, going back, as we have seen, to the beginnings of humanity. When he was about to begin his public ministry, John the Baptist pointed him out with the words: 'Look, there is the lamb of God.' This might seem an extraordinary way of describing someone, but to the Jews at the time, it immediately conjured up one thing: the lamb to be used in sacrifice at Passover time. Then, some three years later, Jesus celebrated the feast of the Passover with his Apostles. Some of the women would have been there helping, with Mary, his mother, ceremoniously lighting the lamps – and Jesus then inserted into this ritual meal an 'extra'. He took some of the unleavened bread and proclaimed that this was his body, his flesh, given for them, and, later, one of the cups of wine he said was his blood, shed for them – the blood of the new covenant. In this way he was replacing the old form of the lamb offered in sacrifice, by himself, offered completely and perfectly to God, his Father.

The Bread of Life

Jesus had paved the way for all this by his teaching earlier, but although the Apostles no doubt recalled it, they must still have found it difficult to accept, let alone understand. Some eighteen months previously, Jesus, immediately after having multiplied the loaves and fish, had told the vast crowd gathered near the lakeside that he would give them the true bread from heaven, which would be himself. Read the whole of John 6 and see how so many found it impossible to accept. First of all the Jews left him, then his own committed disciples, and, finally, only the twelve Apostles were left. Jesus turns to them, and with profound sadness asks them, 'What about you, do you want to go away too?' (John 6:67) How, they felt, could he possibly give them his flesh to eat and his blood to drink (John 6:53–58)? Eating flesh was cannibalism, but for the Jews, drinking blood was even worse because of their belief concerning the sacredness of blood as liquid life.

After celebrating the Passover feast with his disciples, and transforming it with these additional signs of bread and wine, which became his Real Presence, Jesus went out to be truly the Lamb destroyed in a complete and perfect offering of his life to the Father. In the first account we have of the Last Supper, written before any of the Gospels, St Paul puts it clearly (1 Corinthians 11:23–27):

> For the tradition I received from the Lord and also handed on to you is that on the night he was betrayed, the Lord Jesus took some bread, and after he had given thanks, he broke it, and he said, 'This is my body, which is for you; do this in remembrance of me.' And in the same way, with the cup after supper, saying, 'This cup is the new covenant in my blood. Whenever you drink it, do this as a memorial of me.'

> Whenever you eat this bread, then, and drink this cup, you are proclaiming the Lord's death until he comes. Therefore anyone who eats the bread or drinks the cup of the Lord unworthily is answerable for the body and blood of the Lord.

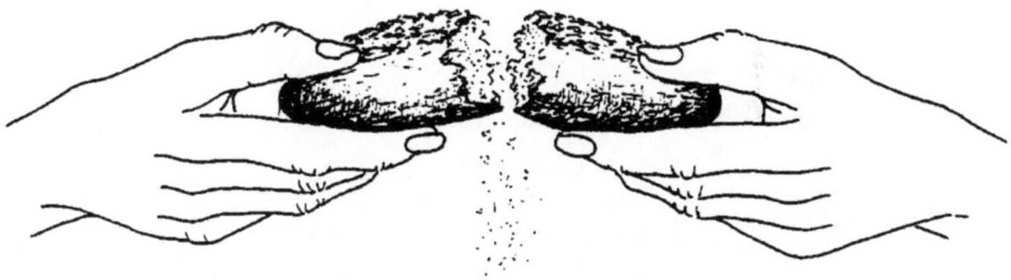

The Perfect Offering

We have looked at the background to the Jewish Passover meal, which Jesus transformed by putting himself in the place of the Passover lamb. Furthermore, the acceptance by the Father of his sacrifice was seen in his Ascension into heaven. The Lord's Supper, as it was then called, came to be the Covenant meal for the followers of Jesus. It was a meal, but at the same time it was a sacrifice, the selfsame sacrifice as that offered on Calvary. In both cases it is Christ offering himself to God, the Father, for us. It is not a new offering, but the same offering made ever-present for us down through the ages until the end of time. Rather as love or respect can be shown in very different ways, so Christ's giving himself in love for us is shown by his Cross and his Last Supper.

Summary

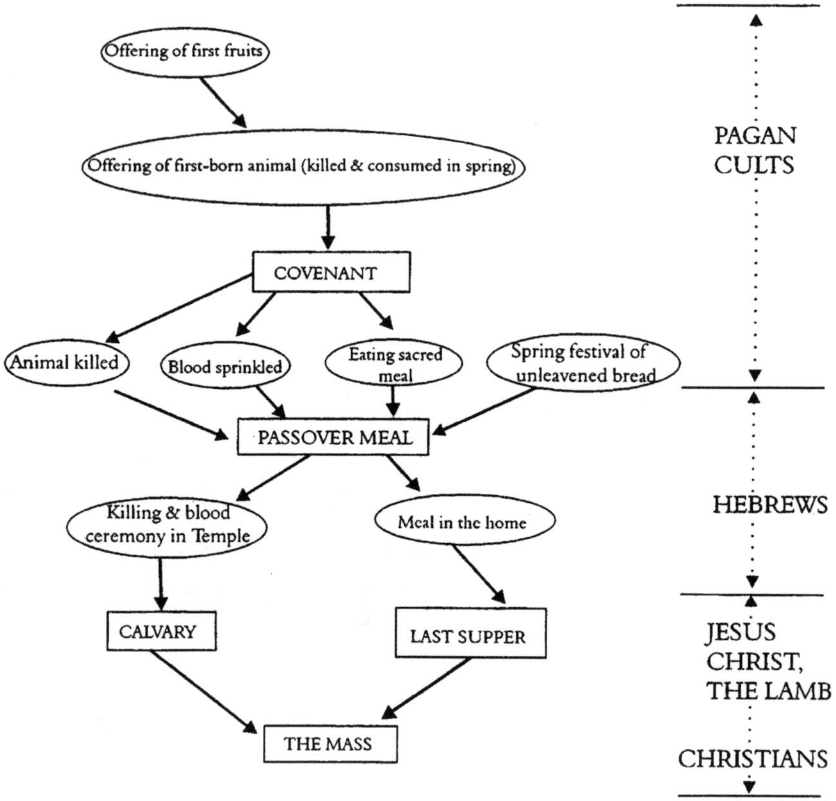
Offering of first fruits
Offering of first-born animal (killed & consumed in spring)
COVENANT
Animal killed
Blood sprinkled
Eating sacred meal
Spring festival of unleavened bread
PASSOVER MEAL
Killing & blood ceremony in Temple
Meal in the home
CALVARY
LAST SUPPER
THE MASS
PAGAN CULTS
HEBREWS
JESUS CHRIST, THE LAMB
CHRISTIANS

✝ *Prayer for this Session and During the Week*

At the end of the Passover Supper, the leader, or head of the family, gives this:

Unto God's gracious mercy and protection we commit ourselves. The Lord bless us and keep us. The Lord make his face to shine upon us and be gracious unto us. The Lord lift up the light of his countenance upon us, and give us peace, both now and evermore. Amen.

(Blessing from Numbers 6:24–26 – adapted)

Shalom, my friend,
shalom my friend, shalom, shalom,
the peace of Christ
I give you today, shalom, shalom.

(Sandra Joan Billington)

Praise God from whom all blessings flow,
praise him, all creatures here below.
Praise him above, ye heavenly host.
Praise Father, Son and Holy Ghost.

? *For Discussion*

Think of the first time you went to Mass. Describe what struck you about it.

What do you find helpful or confusing about Mass?

Scripture Reading

Exodus 12
John 6
1 Corinthians 11

For Further Reading

Read the text of, or better, take part in, a Christian Passover Supper.

Chapter Twenty
The Eucharist: The Real Presence

We have seen how the Mass originated and how Jesus spoke of that complete gift of himself to the Father for us; and, furthermore, how he willed to give himself to us as food.

The Body of Christ

In the early Church the term 'Body of Christ' was understood in the sense of the Risen Christ, the Church or the Eucharist. There was an identity between them. However, after some centuries had passed, attempts were made to distinguish between these. As always with any change, many protested against dividing what the Church had always held as one. Variations in belief arose: an over-spiritual idea of the Eucharist – it was a mere sign; and, with others, an over-materialistic notion – bleeding Hosts and so forth.

However, we know from the writings of the early fathers of the Church and others throughout history, that there was a consistent belief in the Eucharist as the Real Presence of Jesus. This is what Jesus himself had proclaimed during his public ministry, and this is what Christians held to.

Transubstantiation

There have been several attempts to present this faith in philosophical or theological language, the most notable, and that which has been officially sanctioned by the Church, being the doctrine of 'transubstantiation'. To use the technical terms, this means that the 'substance' of the bread and wine has been changed into the Real Presence of Jesus, whilst the 'accidents' (that is, the texture, taste, appearance and so forth) remain the same. However, don't worry if you don't find this particularly helpful!

Real Presence

There is a danger with the above approach of looking upon the Eucharist as 'a thing', whereas it is a personal encounter between Jesus and us. What, then, do we mean by 'Real Presence'? We mean:

1) A fully personal presence which is active and communicative (not like two people asleep in a hospital ward, or strangers standing side by side on a rush-hour train).
2) This presence is real in the sense that it is:
   a) In spirit (that is, it exists even when two people are physically separated).

b) In sign (that is, there is an outward sign of this communication).
c) In the body.

These three forms of personal presence exist in the case of the Eucharist. However, unlike other forms of presence, it is not local, that is, occupying space. The Body of Christ in the Eucharist is his glorified Body and does not occupy space as ours does. It is not limited by the laws of nature. On the other hand, it does not exist everywhere. It exists only where Christ wills to be. A link of presence comes about between the bread and wine on the one hand, and the body and blood of Christ on the other. Someone once described it as the 'collision of God with man'. It is a real presence, a sacramental presence, a glorified presence.

A Further Help

For some, this may seen difficult to follow. Perhaps a simpler way of looking at it is to think of the following. An idea, a thought, may be expressed in several different ways. It may be expressed as a spoken word, or as the tapping out of Morse code, or in sign language, as for a deaf person. In a similar way, Jesus may be truly present in the Eucharist or, in a different manner, in a poor person needing help, or in someone who is dying.

What is important for us is to be joined to him, to be united with him, as a branch to the vine. Without him, we can do nothing. This is why Catholics set such store by receiving Holy Communion frequently.

Adoration and Communion

In the early Church, reservation of the Eucharist was for Communion, and not for adoration. You could take the Eucharist home with you or take it with you on a long journey as a sort of protection, and also to be able to give yourself Communion en route. It could be taken to the sick and to prisoners. However, by the tenth century, there was in the Church a greater emphasis on Christ's divinity (anti-Arian reaction), and this led to a loss of familiarity with the Eucharist and much less frequent Communion. As a result, there was also a switch from Communion to adoration; the altar became distant from the people; Communion was received under one kind and in the mouth, rather than the hand, and only received once or twice a year; the priest had his back to the people and much of the Mass was *sotto voce* in Latin. The Mass became merely a means to produce a Presence for people to adore.

The New Covenant

It is the 'new covenant' of Christ in his blood, and when we take part in this we enter, once again, into a wonderful relationship with God, our Father, through Christ. The sealing of this covenant for us is the great 'Amen' at the end of the Eucharistic Prayer, when the outward sign of that offering of Christ to his Father is seen in the priest raising the bread and wine, now changed into the Real Presence of Jesus, and 'giving' them to God, prior to our receiving that sacred food in Holy Communion.

Further Changes

At the beginning of this century, Pope Saint Pius X advocated frequent communion. This was to give an enormous impetus to further change, which has gone on increasingly during this century. The fact that there have been many changes in recent years and less rigidity in the presentation of the liturgy, has meant that we find different priests and different parishes with differing customs. Furthermore, Mass can be celebrated with great colour and music and ceremony, in a parish church with a cross-section of people of different class, colour, age and degree of commitment, many struggling with the singing and the demand for participation, or, again, very simply, around the table in someone's house, or at the bedside of a sick person. In all these cases, it is the same Mass, the same offering of Christ to the Father and giving of himself to us.

As with much connected with our faith, many of the externals have changed over the years. There may well be some of these that we don't particularly like. However this may be, it is always important to be disciplined and regular in our taking part in the Sunday Mass. One of today's biggest heresies is to do only what we feel like doing. We often don't feel like getting up in the morning or preparing a meal... but we discipline ourselves, and, in the case of the Mass, if we almost force ourselves at times to praise God and to go to Mass, we find that our hearts and minds are enlarged; we are different and we are caught up in a world of praise.

The Externals

At Mass, the priest wears special clothes called vestments, because he is taking the place of Christ and doing something that is very special. The colours of the vestments have a meaning:

WHITE	Sign of joy and purity. It is used for many of Our Lord's feasts, as well as Our Lady's, and other notable occasions.
RED	Colour of fire and blood. Used in Masses of the Holy Spirit, on feasts of martyrs and on Good Friday.
PURPLE	Penitential and also used for mourning.

GREEN Symbolises hope and is used on Sundays through the year, because Sunday is a special day for keeping alive our hope in the Resurrection.

Liturgical Year

The whole year is divided up so that we are able to remember better the different aspects of God's love for us and what we can do to respond to this. The pivot and centre is, of course, EASTER, the feast of the Resurrection, which occurred on the first day of the week. It is precisely for this reason that we go to Mass and communicate with the resurrected Christ on every first day of the week, if this is possible.

The six weeks before Easter are known as Lent, and the seven weeks following Easter lead into the birthday of the Church, Pentecost. In addition to this, we have the celebration of Christ's birth at Christmas, preceded by four weeks of preparation (Advent), and followed by nearly two weeks leading up to Epiphany.

This does not cover the whole year, so to fill in all the other Sundays, the Church numbers them 'Sundays of the Year', and they fill in the gap between Epiphany and Lent, and then again between Pentecost and Advent. There are thirty-four altogether.

Readings

The Vatican Council recommended that there should be more readings from Scripture at Mass, and that they should be varied and suitable – 'richer fare should be provided for the faithful at the table of God's Word'. This has been brought about by having a three year cycle of readings for Sundays and big feast days. Furthermore, on these days there should normally be three readings: from the Old Testament, from the New Testament and from the Gospel.

For the seasons of Advent, Christmas, Epiphany, Lent, Easter and Pentecost, the readings concern the theme of the season, but for the remaining thirty-four Sundays of the year, it is different. On these latter, the second reading (usually an epistle) and the Gospel are more or less continuous from Sunday to Sunday, and the Old Testament reading is chosen to harmonise with the Gospel.

The year is divided in this way to help us recall the essentials of our faith in and attachment to Christ, and it matters not at all, in fact, whether Christ was actually born in December, whether or not it was exactly seven weeks from Easter to Pentecost and so forth. These are signs of an underlying historical truth and reality.

All the other feasts celebrated during the year, highlighting other aspects in the life of Jesus, or of Our Lady or the saints, point to God's love for us and are to help us poor mortals respond in a better way to that love.

✝ *Prayers for this Session and During the Week*

Soul of my Saviour
sanctify my breast;
Body of Christ,
be thou my saving guest.
Blood of my Saviour,
bathe me in thy tide,
wash me with water
flowing from thy side.

Strength and protection
may thy Passion be;
O Blessed Jesus
hear and answer me;
deep in thy wounds, Lord,
hide and shelter me;
so shall I never,
never part from thee.

Guard and defend me
from the foe malign;
in death's dread moments
make me only thine;
call me, and bid me
come to thee on high
when I may praise thee
with thy saints for aye.

(Ascribed to John XXII, 1249–1334,
tr. anonymous)

I am the bread of life,
He who comes to me
will never be hungry.
I will raise him up.
I will raise him up.
I will raise him up to eternal life.
I am the bread of life.

I am the spring of life
He who hopes in me
will never be thirsty.
I will raise him up.
I will raise him up.
I will raise him up to eternal life.
I am the spring of life.

I am the way of life.
He who follows me
will never be lonely.
I will raise him up.
I will raise him up.
I will raise him up to eternal life.
I am the way of life.
I am the truth of life.
He who looks for me
will never seek blindly.
I will raise him up.
I will raise him up.
I will raise him up to eternal life.
I am the truth of life.

I am the life of life.
He who dies with me
will never die vainly.
I will raise him up.
I will raise him up.

I will raise him up to eternal life.
I am the life of life.

(David Konstant)

? For Discussion

Why do you think the Sunday Mass is so important to Catholics?

Scripture Reading

John 6; 14:6; 15:4–5
1 John 4:16
1 Corinthians 11:26

For Further Reading

The Sunday Missal

Chapter Twenty-One
Love in Action: Christian Morality

St Augustine once said, 'Love, and do what you like'. One difficulty with taking this at face value is that the interpretation of 'love' can be so varied. Therefore we need some guidelines. In his teaching, Jesus gave us just these. Furthermore, he promised the guidance of his Holy Spirit of love to lead his followers into all truth – a guarantee to his Church to be free of error, 'the gates of the underworld can never overpower it.' (Matthew 16:18)

The Moral Law

Very briefly, we are now going to look at the ways in which our love for others should be shown on the wide canvas of the world and then in the person-to-person situation of our lives. All good, as well as all evil, has its origin in our mind, our thoughts, in our hearts and our emotions. This is where love originates, and so it is important that our ideas, our attitudes and our feelings are well oriented in all the areas we are going to touch on. It has been said that Jesus's teaching is a compass rather than an Ordnance map. This means that both the teachings of Jesus and those of the Church, under the impulsion of the Holy Spirit, are more concerned with principles than with detailed precepts. The role of the Church is to make more explicit God's love offered to all.

Principles

What, then, are the principles for us to follow in order to apply the law of love? The first is that we need to be as aware as possible of the facts and circumstances surrounding a problem. Secondly, we look at possible courses of action, with the reasons for them, our intention, and, finally, after thought and prayer, guided by the teaching of the Church and our own conscience, we make a decision. The sections that follow vary considerably in length. This is in no way whatsoever an indication of their relative importance.

THE WORLD'S RESOURCES

Pope Paul VI coined the phrase, 'If you want peace, work for justice.' As long ago as 1972, Archbishop Camara said, in his forthright way, that 'true Christianity rejects the idea that some are born poor and others rich, and that the poor must attribute their poverty to the will of God, when it is injustices between man which are our real problem to be resolved by man, knowing that Christ wants us all to live humanly as befits man, neither sub-humanised by misery, or de-humanised by riches!'

One of the major practical problems is the insistence by the richer countries on debt servicing by the poor countries of the world, thus strangling their already tottering economies. Furthermore, conditions are imposed on debtor countries which contribute, at least in the short term, to recession, unemployment and a drastic lowering of living standards. In these and allied matters, the Church's role is to 'illuminate the conscience of decision makers... the burden should not fall disproportionately on poor countries. Within poor countries, the burden should not fall disproportionately on the poor. It is morally wrong to deprive a nation of the means to meet the basic needs of its people in order to repay debt.' This is summed up in a short story that comes from Korea.

There is a legend from the East that tells of a brave warrior who died, came before the gates of eternity, and was given the option of choosing to go to heaven or hell. First, he decided to visit hell and, upon entering, discovered a large table laden with exotic dishes. But the people seated at the table had very glum expressions on their faces. On asking why they were sad, he was told that the only rule in hell was that all food had to be eaten with ten foot long chopsticks.

The warrior, unhappy at the prospect of hell, then went to heaven. Here, he discovered a similar banquet, but this time, the people were happy. Asking whether the rule of eating was different, he was told that folk in heaven have to eat with the similar long sticks, but that they had learned to feed one another across the table, instead of trying to feed themselves.

(Author Unknown)

The World Health Organisation warned us in 1995 that poverty is the leading cause of premature death and ill health across the planet, and that the gaps between rich and poor are widening, not closing. More than one fifth of the 5.6 billion people in the world live in extreme poverty, almost one third of the world's children are under-nourished, and half the global population lacks access to essential drugs.

PEACE AND WAR

The peace between countries, for which we so frequently pray, is more than just the silence of guns. It involves justice, and that is closely tied to the whole question of the countless billions of pounds spent on armaments.

The whole question of world peace finds its roots, of course, in the individual. Two stories illustrate this.

The first is the story of Abraham Lincoln, who was seen one day walking along the road holding the hands of two small boys.

A neighbour was passing and asked, 'What's the matter, Mr Lincoln, with the boys?'

'Just what's the matter with the whole world,' replied Lincoln. 'I've got three walnuts and each wants two.'

The other is of a woman who tells her friend that a particular flower is beautiful.

The friend says, 'What flower?'

'That flower.'

'You mean that weed? That! It's not a flower, it's a weed! And it's ugly!'

Hatred suddenly fills the mind of the first person, who loved her flower, and she takes a gun and shoots the friend, but then immediately says, 'I didn't want to do that, but I have a commitment to flowers.'

Possessions and possessiveness are the two greatest reasons for the lack of peace – both in the individual and in society.

The Vatican Council stated clearly that all warfare which tends indiscriminately to the destruction of entire cities or wide areas with their inhabitants is a crime against God and man, to be firmly and unhesitatingly condemned (*Gaudium et Spes*, para. 80). Pope John XXIII called for the banning of all nuclear weapons. Several times he stated very clearly that a deterrent based on the nuclear threat can only be temporarily justified or morally acceptable whilst negotiations for disarmament are being seriously pursued. Many bishops throughout the world have come out even more strongly, not only against the use of a nuclear deterrent, but also against any policy of deterrence. On Peace Sunday, 1988, Bishop Thomas of Northampton said:

> Can we really set ourselves up seriously in a position where we are prepared to use these weapons in certain circumstances? It seems to me we adopt a position there that is immoral too. It is this threat of mutual destruction. If you do this, or that happens, then we are going to let loose these weapons. It is a serious stance that you take, that you are prepared to do this, and, in certain circumstances, will do it. And if I believe that the use of these weapons is immoral, then I believe myself, I'm convinced, that such a policy, such a stance, is immoral too.

It is true to say that, over the centuries, the Church's attitude to war has been steadily hardening, and the very different conditions today make it increasingly difficult to justify any war. Can the traditional conditions for a just war (that is to say, a just cause, a lawful method, every other means to a just solution having failed, and the good effects sought far outweighing the consequences of warfare) ever be acceptable?

INVOLVEMENT IN PUBLIC LIFE

Some are called to this, and there is a need everywhere for more committed lay people to be involved in civic and political decision-making. You may have read of the story of Hilaire Belloc when he put up as a candidate in the General Election of 1906. He stood as a Liberal against the Tories, who had a majority at the previous election. At his adoption meeting, Belloc had told the local Liberal Council: 'My religion is of course of greater moment to me by far than my politics,' and he would always put his religion first if he had to choose. They had adopted him unanimously as their candidate, but still it was bound to tell against him heavily that he was a Catholic and a French citizen by birth. 'Don't vote for a Frenchman and a Catholic,' was the Tory slogan.

Belloc held his first election campaign meeting in the schools of the Catholic Cathedral. Even the clergy warned him that the religious question was going to be very tricky for him, and that he had better say nothing about it. He proudly disregarded their advice. He rose to address the packed audience and spoke as follows:

> Gentlemen, I am a Catholic. As far as possible I go to Mass every day. This [taking a rosary out of his pocket] is a rosary. As far as possible, I kneel down and tell these beads every day. If you reject me on account of my religion I shall thank God that he has spared me the indignity of being your representative!'

There was a hush of astonishment, followed by a thunderclap of applause; and in the end he defeated his opponent by a considerable majority!

Of course, there is less opposition to Catholicism today than there was then, and perhaps it is because of this that we have lost some of the fervour of those days.

Many laws and regulations of the state touch on the moral order; here the Church cannot remain silent and individual Catholics must speak out. This has already been indicated in the previous two sections. It is daily more and more imperative that a Christlike voice is heard, that statements are made not only by Church leaders, as frequently happens, but also that individuals speak out, write letters to their MPs and to the papers, get on to local radio, go to meetings and so on.

It has been said that if a lot of little people do a lot of little things, then the result is very large. Many great movements and happenings have begun in a very small way. Take, for example, the way Amnesty International began.

PRISONERS OF CONSCIENCE

In November 1960, two students were sitting in a cafe in Lisbon, talking. They got on to politics and lifted their glasses, toasting 'freedom'. It was under Salazar's dictatorship, and they were spotted by the police, arrested and sentenced to seven years in prison. An English Catholic lawyer saw a report of this in a London paper and wondered how the Portuguese authorities could be persuaded to release them. He hit on the idea of bombarding Salazar with written protests – and it worked. This Catholic lawyer was Peter Benenson, and he and two friends decided to launch an appeal to work for the release of all those imprisoned for their opinions (political or religious) – prisoners of conscience (but *not* those imprisoned for using violence: the IRA, for example). The appeal was launched with an article in *The Observer* on Trinity Sunday 1961, and that was the beginning of Amnesty International.

POVERTY, UNEMPLOYMENT AND HOMELESSNESS

These problems, we know only too well, exist here in our own country, though perhaps not nearly so acutely as in the Third World.

Mother Teresa, on one of her visits to London, remarked: 'Here in Britain you have a different kind of poverty: a poverty of loneliness and of being unwanted, a poverty of spirit – and that is the worst disease in the world today.'

Whilst the Church does all it can to alleviate these ills through many of its societies and organisations, the excessively competitive and selfish world in which we live continues to aggravate the situation. We can all learn something from the story of the contented fisherman.

The rich industrialist from the North was horrified to find the Southern fisherman lying lazily beside his boat, smoking a pipe. 'Why aren't you out fishing?' said the industrialist.

'Because I have caught enough fish for the day,' said the fisherman.

'Why don't you catch more than you need?' said the industrialist.

'What would I do with it?' asked the fisherman.

'You could earn more money,' was the reply. 'With that you could have a motor fixed to your boat. Then you could go into deeper waters and catch more fish. Then you would make enough to buy nylon nets. These would bring you more fish and more money. Soon you would have enough money to own two boats... maybe even a fleet of boats. Then you would be a rich man like me.'

'What would I do then?' asked the fisherman.

'Then you could sit down and enjoy life,' said the industrialist.

'What do you think I am doing right now?' said the contented fisherman.

(Father de Mello)

Linked with this whole topic is the question of a just wage. This must be determined so that the worker is paid a wage which allows him to live a truly human life and fulfil any family obligations in a worthy manner. Other factors which enter in are the contribution he makes to the production, the financial state of the concern for which he works and the requirements of the general good of the country and the world at large (see Pope John XXIII's encyclical, *Mater et Magistra*).

Strikes are considered a legitimate but extreme means to attempt to bring about justice. The right to strike, however, must always be related to the common good of society, and not the particular interest of a small section of that society.

CAPITAL PUNISHMENT

This is a complex question, but it would seem that if we take into account some of the principles we have been considering – God's unbounded love and mercy, the value and respect due to all human life, and the injunction not to kill – then, provided the common good is also respected, final judgement must be reserved to God alone. However, this also raises the whole question of punitive justice, the workings of our legal system and the state of our prison system...

RESPECT FOR LIFE FROM CONCEPTION TO THE COFFIN

All that has been said so far could in fact come under this heading. However, our concern here is for the individual human life, particularly in its most helpless form. Many today are messing about with human life in the hope eventually of bringing about Huxley's *Brave New World* in which the handicapped, the unintelligent and the misfits are eliminated.

We are well on the way to experiencing this 'biological time bomb', more devastating in many ways than any nuclear explosion.

Techniques are practised enabling couples to have children who were not able to do so:

1) artificial insemination: where sperm is injected into the womb, usually by use of a syringe. This enables a couple to have children if, for example, the husband is paralysed (artificial insemination by the husband: AIH). If the husband is infertile, another man's sperm may be used (artificial insemination by donor: AID).
2) in vitro fertilisation (IVF): this involves fertilisation outside of the womb, the human embryo later being inserted in the womb. Again, the sperm may or may not come from the husband; indeed the ovum need not come from the wife, so that three parties may be involved: the generic parents and the child-bearer.

The Church expresses great caution concerning AIH, and strong opposition to AID and IVF, for the following reasons.

The importance of the family: the Church has always upheld the fundamental social unit. A particular strength of the family is that the parents bring life into the world through an act of mutual love and self-giving: for growth and wholeness, human life should come from an act of human love. To separate procreation from the sexual act, which is what these techniques must involve, could have grave repercussions on our society's understanding of the family. The psychological effects of this separation on the family itself may also be very serious.

The introduction of a third party in the case of AID, and most treatments involving IVF, presents another attack on the family as traditionally understood. This clearly contravenes the Church's teaching that sexual relations be confined to married couples. The donation of sperm from a person other than the husband is simply another form of adultery.

With IVF, as already stated, the sperm and ova of a couple may be fertilised and the embryo placed in the womb of another woman. The moral problems arising from such an arrangement are obvious. A child could possess a multiplicity of parents, which is clearly damaging to any understanding of family.

Thus, all these techniques, to different degrees, undermine family life, and could create a generation of deeply insecure people, unsure of where they came from and to whom they belong.

Furthermore, the embryo is 'a human being with potential', and the experimentation with, discarding and killing of them, is totally unacceptable, as it constitutes a further serious erosion of respect for the sanctity of life and of love.

Abortion also is condemned for a similar reason; so are euthanasia and racism. All are concerned with human life and love and respect. The Church has declared quite clearly, that 'from the time that the ovum is fertilised, a life is begun which is neither that of the father nor of the mother; it is rather the life of a new human being with its own growth'. Cardinal Hume has added to this.

> Conception is a unique biological event in the creation of a human. Science has demonstrated that from the moment of conception there is established in the cell the generic programme of a living being which is human. I understand that biologically there is no comparable decisive milestone in development

> until birth itself. For that reason alone this new life demands unconditional respect and protection.
>
> (A statement by Cardinal Hume printed in *Briefing*, 20th March 1987)

With euthanasia, this is not a case of refusing to use extraordinary methods to conquer a critical condition in a patient already suffering from chronic terminal illness. To help a person to die in peace and dignity is part of the art of medicine and of nursing, and in terminal care it is quite in order to endeavour, through drugs and so on, to keep ahead of the pain, even if at some point this may hasten the moment of death.

In other words, it is not necessary to continue to prolong the process of dying. But it is certainly not morally permissible to do anything which will directly bring on death.

Much talked about questions concerning contraception, masturbation, homosexuality and suchlike are usually, in some way or another, failures to love as openly and as unselfishly as we should.

Climbing the Mountain

In all the areas we have been considering, there is often no easy, straightforward answer. Putting God's love into effect in our daily lives and in the problem situations we all encounter, is like going up a mountain – we often stumble and perhaps fall, but hopefully we don't give up. We still want to continue the journey, and Jesus is accompanying us with hand outstretched to hold us and guide us. It is only if we turn around, as it were, wishing to have no more to do with the climb, and start heading downhill, that we separate ourselves from God. Provided we keep hold of the whole idea of going up the mountain, of believing in God's love for us, of trying to follow his way, of being ready to repent and start again when we fail, then we need have no fear.

The wife of the writer C.S. Lewis once told a delightful story of an old African chief who listened patiently for some time to a missionary who, in explaining the Christian faith, seemed to stress the 'Thou shalt nots'.

'I do not understand,' replied the old native. 'You tell me that I must not take my neighbour's wife.'

'That's right,' said the missionary.

'Nor his ivory, nor his oxen.'

'Quite right.'

'And I must not dance the war dance and then ambush him on the trail and kill him.'

'That's it.'

'But I cannot do any of these things!' said the old man. 'I am too old. So,' concluded the chief, 'to be old and to be a Christian, they are the same thing!'

You see, Christ didn't give us a lot of 'do nots'; he said, 'Love God, and love your neighbour as yourself.' That is his way. That is the ideal, and, slowly and painfully, as we are faithful to our daily time of prayer, and, as Catholics, of frequenting the sacraments, we journey up the mountain and grow in showing forth God's love through all that we do and all that we are. Think also of the following story, again, one of Anthony de Mello's.

THE DIAMOND

The wise man had reached the outskirts of the village and settled down under a tree for the night, when a villager came running up to him and said, 'The stone! The stone! Give me the precious stone!'

'What stone?' asked the wise man.

'Last night the Lord Shiva appeared to me in a dream,' said the villager, 'and told me that if I went to the outskirts of the village at dusk I should find a wise man who would give me a precious stone that would make me rich for ever.'

The wise man rummaged in his bag and pulled out a stone. 'He probably meant this one,' he said, as he handed the stone over to the villager. 'I found it on a forest path some days ago. You can certainly have it.'

The man looked at the stone in wonder. It was a diamond. Probably the largest diamond in the whole world, for it was as large as a man's head.

He took the diamond and walked away. All night he tossed about in bed, unable to sleep. Next day, at the crack of dawn, he woke the wise man and said, 'Give me the wealth that makes it possible for you to give this diamond away so easily.'

✠ *Prayers for this Session and During the Week*

Christ has no body now on earth but yours,
no hands but yours
no feet but yours.
Yours are the eyes through which must look out
Christ's compassion on the world.
Yours are the feet with which he is to go about doing good.
Yours are the hands with which he blesses now.

(St Teresa of Avila)

Lead me from Death to Life from Falsehood to Truth.
Lead me from Despair to Hope from Fear to Trust.
Lead me from Hate to Love from War to Peace.
Let Peace fill our Heart our World, our Universe.
Peace Peace Peace.

(Origin Unknown)

? *For Discussion*

What do we really need, what could be dispensed with, and what do we waste? How can I share more with those in need? ('Live simply, that others may simply live'.)

What can we do to help those faced with different moral decisions? Give examples from experience.

Scripture Reading

Matthew 25:31–46

For Further Reading

Catholic Social Teaching by Theodor Herr (New City)

Moral Dilemmas by Gerald Vann (Collins)

Caroline Chisholm – the Emigrant's Friend by Joanna Bogle (Gracewing)

Chapter Twenty-Two
Rebirth: Death and After

The theological term for this – death, judgement, heaven and hell – is eschatology, from two Greek words which mean 'last' and 'discourse'. In a sense it means the final harvest – the whole perspective; the world as having a purpose to be accomplished and, at the same time, as containing within itself seeds of that accomplishment.

Death

There are two moments in our lives of which we can be absolutely certain: the present moment, and the moment of our death. In the prayer to Our Lady that we say the most often, the Hail Mary, we ask for her intercession for us at precisely these times.

Some years ago at a headmasters conference, those taking part fell to discussing the purpose of education. After a while, some of the non-Catholic heads turned to Father Paul Neville, who was headmaster of Ampleforth, and asked him what he thought: 'Well,' he commented, 'we educate our boys for death!'

Death is the climax of our lives, and, in many ways, the most important moment. In a certain sense it is the completion of our baptism. We are baptised into the death and Resurrection of Jesus Christ. A reminder of this is the Easter candle that stands by the font at baptism. It also stands by the coffin at a funeral. We begin our lives by receiving everything. We end our lives on this earth, hopefully, by giving everything, by the total gift of ourselves. The journey through life towards our death is a journey, a growth in loving ourselves, which means possessing ourselves, in order to give ourselves to others and to God. We can only love others if we love ourselves, and it has been said that only if we accept the fact of our death can we begin to live, and to love.

Any fear of death that we may have, with most people, is associated with the thought of suffering which may precede it. People who have had a near-death experience have described it in very positive terms.

Gwen Ffrangcon-Davies, a well-known actress in the early part of the century, was interviewed on television at the age of ninety-seven. She was partially sighted, and the interviewer had visited her in her cottage in the country. She was seen on-screen walking barefoot across the lawn, guided by the interviewer.

'I love the feel of the grass beneath my feet,' remarked Gwen.

The interviewer then, with slight hesitation, asked: 'Well, Miss Davies, you must at your age have thought of death. Are you afraid of death?'

Gwen Ffrangcon-Davies paused for a second and then, with a thoughtful smile, replied: 'Well, I suppose you're always a little nervous of doing something for the first time.'

Bereavement

Probably the greater suffering involved is that of the bereaved who have been close in love to the deceased. This suffering often passes through several stages – numbness, disbelief, grief, anger (often directed towards the medical profession or the clergy), guilt ('If only I had...'), searching and sometimes apathy and depression. Most people experience several or all of these stages over the couple of months following the death of a loved one. The wound of bereavement becomes, with time, less acute, but is never totally healed.

Judgement

Perhaps there are some who will also fear the thought of judgement. We believe that there will be a particular judgement at the moment of death. It will be rather like being born again out of the womb, and held up so as to see God, face to face; and, in seeing God as he is, we also see ourselves as we are.

In a country churchyard, one of the tombstones has this inscription:

> Remember man that passeth by, as thou art now, so once was I; And as I am so thou must be; prepare thyself to follow me.

A visitor has added underneath:

> To follow thee's not my intent, unless I know which way thou went.

Given that our overall orientation is directed to God, then, unlike the above visitor, we need have no fear.

Purgatory

However, because none of us are completely ready for that final union with God, that total binding in love with our Creator, we need to be brought, as it were, to the right fusion temperature. This is what we call purgatory, a purifying process.

Just as we help and support one another in our prayer in this life, so we can continue helping those who have died. We pray for those who have died that they may 'quickly' pass through that purifying stage of purgatory. However, on our timescale, it is instantaneous. Once death has occurred, the person is beyond space and time in a state that our finite minds cannot grasp.

Hell

A total and complete rejection of God and all that is good would result in a person going to hell. Yes, it does exist. Jesus spoke of it on a number of occasions (Matthew 25:41–46 and so on). Someone whose will is turned away from God totally, who rejects whatever he knows of God or what is seen to be good, and who does this knowing fully what he is doing – that person is oriented to hell, which is the absence of God, of love, of life (1 John 3:14).

Artists and visionaries throughout the ages have attempted to portray the world of the spirit, but it is only possible to give very inadequate pointers expressed in terms of the things of this world. One is reminded of the story of a preacher in the West Indies who was trying to describe hell to his congregation:

> 'You all is seen molten iron runnin' out from a furnace, ain't you?' he asked. The congregation said it had. 'Well,' continued the preacher, 'dey uses dat stuff for ice cream in de place what I'm talkin' 'bout.'

We rightly discard such comparisons, but we must not make the mistake of disregarding the truth of the existence of hell, although we can never presume to know or guess whether or not there is anyone in that state.

Heaven

We now come to the happier state of heaven. Our biggest difficulty in attempting to think of any of these questions is that we cannot, with our finite minds, conceive a state of being 'outside' time. All our thought is expressed in space–time language. The word just used, 'outside' is a 'space' word. What can we say, then, about eternity, timelessness?

Firstly, it is *not* time just going on and on for ever. That would be nearer to hell! It is more like time condensed so much that it no longer exists. For example, if you are doing something which completely absorbs your interest, or greatly enjoying the company of someone you love, you fail to notice the hours passing: a day can seem like a few minutes. This is the nearest we can come to thinking of eternity – intensity of loving. On the other hand, if you are engaged in some task that you find difficult and boring, that day can seem like weeks, and this would be a pointer to what hell might be like. 'Duration' after death, then, is of a higher order than that of our time, and eternal life does not mean eternal boredom!

Secondly, heaven is not a geographical location – a big dreamland with pink clouds, halos, wings, pearly gates and alabaster streets! Heaven is the experience and the celebration of love. Not all wedding receptions are happy occasions, but, nevertheless, Jesus does give a wedding feast as an example of what heaven will be like (Matthew 22:2). To the extent, then, that we love one another unselfishly now, so we will be united with one another in the next life – caught up completely in that movement of love that is God.

The End of Time

We are very conscious today that the human race is a unity and that the destiny of each of us is bound up with the destiny of society. We want the human race to survive and progress: hence our concern about pollution, world resources and suchlike. So when we think of 'the end of the world', we think of it in the sense of achievement and purpose. This is the work of the Holy Spirit acting through us. This is also why we would disagree with people like Jehovah's Witnesses who look forward to a sudden cataclysmic end to the world. I once saw a photo of a man bearing a sandwich-board on which was written in big letters: 'The end of the world is near.' The man was in the process of peering at the sign on the bus stop: 'Times of last buses'!

Jesus has revealed to us that he will come again in glory. We proclaim in our liturgy, 'Christ has died; Christ is risen; Christ will come again.' This will mark the glorification and transformation of all creation and the final judgement. The nature of our glorified body is a mystery. Certainly it will be different from our present body and, similarly, the whole creation will be changed.

Pierre Teilhard de Chardin, a great priest, theologian and scientist, sets the whole of creation, and hence its final end and purpose, in relation to Christ.

> God did not will individually (nor could he have constructed as though they were separate bits) the sun, the earth, plants, or man. He willed his Christ; and in order to have his Christ, he had to create the spiritual world, and man in particular, upon which Christ might germinate; and to have man, he had to launch the vast process of organic life (which, accordingly, is not a superfluity but an essential organ of the world); and the birth of that organic life called for the entire cosmic turbulence.
>
> (Pierre Teilhard de Chardin, *Science and Christ*, Collins and Harper, 1968, p.79)

Conclusion

To conclude this section, I leave with you two quotations. The first is a short passage from de Caussade's book, *Self-Abandonment to Divine Providence*; and the second is a poem written by a fifteen year old on the death of her grandfather.

> The fear of death and the judgement is good provided it does not go so far as to trouble and disturb you; if it did it would be an illusion of the devil. After all, why should you be troubled? Because you have not yet done what you have not been able to do? Does God demand the impossible?... Without counting in any way on ourselves, we must try to accomplish all that he asks of us and hope only in his goodness and the merits of Jesus Christ his Son.

DEATH

If death was a colour, it would be white;
because I believe that when you die, you go to a place
    which is very peaceful, and you are
eternally happy.

If death was an animal, it would be a dove;
because they are represented as peace animals and I
    believe when you die, you are released
from your body and become a free spirit.

If death was a time of day, it would be midnight;
when most people are quiet, because I think death is silent.
    It is also midnight because it is a
beginning of a new day, a new life.

If death was a place, it would be somewhere very quiet and
    peaceful, like a church;
because I think church represents Heaven.

If death was a type of weather, it would be snowy;
because it is white and when it settles, it looks really lovely.

If death was a sound, it would be silent;
because that is what the end of one's life sounds like.

I feel that death is nothing to be frightened about and that it is very peaceful unlike earth.
I also feel that Granddad is happy, no longer in pain, nor is he suffering. He has taken our
love with him, and so he will be loved forever.

✟ *Prayer for this Session and During the Week*

Imagine being seated in church after your death with your coffin in front of the altar. Who are the people gathered at your funeral? What is the priest saying about you? Later in the day, what are the mourners saying about you as they leave the cemetery or crematorium?

We seem to give them back to Thee, O God, who gavest them to us. Yet as Thou didst not lose them in giving, so do we not lose them by their return. Not as the world giveth, givest Thou, O Lover of souls. What Thou givest, Thou takest not away, for what is thine is ours also if we are Thine. And life is eternal, and love is immortal, and death is only an horizon, and an horizon is nothing, save the limit of our sight. Lift us up, strong Son of God, that we may see further; cleanse our eyes that we may see more clearly; draw us closer to Thyself that we may know ourselves to be nearer to our loved ones who are with Thee. And while Thou dost prepare a place for us, prepare us also for that happy place, that where Thou art we may be also for evermore.

(Prayer used by Fr. Bede Jarrett, OP)

? *For Discussion*

How do you look upon death?
How would you like to meet Jesus at the moment of death?

Scripture Reading

Matthew 25: the whole chapter, but especially verses 31–46
1 Corinthians 15: the whole chapter, but especially verses 35–58

For Further Reading

Hope for the Flowers by Trina Paulns (Paulist Press)

Chapter Twenty-Three
The Church through the Centuries

We saw in a previous session (chapter ten) that one of Jesus's main works was to gather together a group of men and send them out to baptise and to teach as he had done. This was the beginning of the Church.

Furthermore, he foretold that it would grow and develop and change: like a tiny mustard seed (Matthew 13:31–32); like the yeast put in the bread to make it rise (Matthew 13:33); it would be, wrote St Paul, like the human body with many parts (1 Corinthians 12:12–30); it would be God's special people called to carry on his work. In all this, Jesus prayed for unity amongst his followers (John 17:20–23).

Early Disputes

Jesus knew so well the nature of man. He knew that when people work together, even under the guidance and impulsion of his Spirit of love, there would be a tendency to disagreements and conflict. He had experienced it even on the occasion of his last celebration of the Passover when he instituted the Eucharist. The mother of James and John had provoked jealousy and argument regarding who was to be the first in the coming Kingdom: Matthew 20:20–23 and Luke 22:24–27.

In the early years, some of the Christians in Jerusalem practised a more rigorous sort of life – a kind of Christian communism, somewhat similar to a monastic order. However, in spite of the rosy picture described by St Luke in the Acts, there were some shadows. The hypocrisy and dishonesty of Ananias is an example (Acts 5:1–11).

Then there was the dispute amongst the early converts, between the Hellenists and the Hebrews (Acts 6:1). The first disciples were mostly of Jewish origin. However, there were two types of Jews: Hebrews – those living in Palestine and keeping the traditions of their ancestors, reading the Bible in Hebrew in the synagogues and so on; and Hellenists – Jews born outside Palestine. The latter were quite numerous and to be found in all the towns around the Mediterranean. They spoke Greek and read the Bible in Greek in their synagogues. In Jerusalem the majority were Hebrews, but there were also to be found Hellenists who had settled down there after a time away. These included Barnabas and all the newly commissioned deacons, who had Greek names (Acts 6:2–6).

Even Paul and Barnabas were in open disagreement at times. However, the most significant area of dispute arose over the question of circumcision and certain other specifically Jewish customs. With the reception of pagans and proselytes (those not of Jewish race, but who had been converted to Judaism) into the Church, the question was whether they too should have to conform to Jewish customs. This dispute led to the gathering of the Apostles and disciples in Jerusalem around AD 51. It was the first council of the Church, and after discussion they agreed that, amongst other things, circumcision was not necessary.

Growth and Division

Through all this, the Church continued to grow. The growth often came through persecution, which led to dispersion of many of the Christians, but this, in turn, led to further evangelisation. Whenever we look at the history of the Church in any age, we must, inevitably, see the transforming power of the Holy Spirit. The early Christians, and particularly the Apostles, were at first frightened people, but their fear changed to courage. We have only to look, for example, at Peter himself at Jesus's trial, and later when preaching to the crowds at Pentecost.

The terrible persecutions by successive Roman Emperors finally gave way to acceptance of Christianity when the Emperor Constantine became Christian in the fourth century. Christianity was by then felt to be a stable force in a disintegrating empire. However, the political division of the Roman Empire: east and west, Constantinople and Rome, being in the hands of Constantine's two sons, together with cultural differences which infiltrated into theology, gradually gave rise to a division within the Church – the Orthodox (the east) and the Latins (the west). Barbarian attacks and the growth of Islam further aggravated the division.

A further 'breakaway' occurred in the sixteenth century. Wealth and corruption had infiltrated into parts of the Church. Some, like Luther and Calvin, in attempting to bring about reform, were like people emptying the dirty water out of the bath and, in so doing, losing the baby as well. In England, it was brought to a head by King Henry VIII's quarrel with the Pope over his marriage problems. This was coupled with his desire for money in order to wage war against Spain, and so he ransacked the convents and monasteries in order to finance his military campaigns.

Spots on the Beautiful Carpet

However, lest all this should appear a somewhat gloomy picture, we must now look at the other side of the coin.

What we have highlighted so far are really a few black spots on the carpet. G.K. Chesterton tells of the man who goes into a beautiful room in a fine house, and all he notices is a dirty mark on the carpet. He fails to see the rest of the carpet, the room or the house. It is true that the dirty mark should not be there, but we must not become hypnotised by it. It is like that with the Church! So, we will now look at some of the wonderful ways that the Church, both human and divine, like its Founder, has shown forth the love and power of God throughout its history. Indeed, it would be true to say that any other organisation would have crumbled and collapsed centuries ago if it had had to endure some of the vicissitudes that have befallen the Catholic Church.

The Whole House

Many of the setbacks that have befallen the Church, and especially the occasions of persecution, have resulted in men and women, ordinary people, rising to great heights of holiness. A few of these have been officially recognised by the Church (canonised) as saints. Saints are thus ordinary people whose love for Christ gave them great love and courage in loving others, and sometimes dying for them. It is good to know details of the lives of some of the saints, as they can be an inspiration to us. Some founded religious orders (for example, Saints Benedict, Dominic, Ignatius and John Bosco), but each one in his or her life highlighted some of the virtues (for example, St Francis of Assisi – poverty and prayer; St Thomas More – joy and fun; St Francis Xavier – spreading the Gospel; St Jean Vianney – humility).

So many unknown ones have contributed to the building up of Christ's Kingdom through the ages. Many, whose vocation has been the upbringing of a family, have been bright lights reflecting Christ's love to others, and have been an inspiration to all around them. Most can probably think of such people amongst their own families and friends.

This brief overview of the history of the Church can be brought to a suitable conclusion with the well-known quotation from Macaulay's 'Essay on Ranke's *History of the Popes*'.

> The Catholic Church is still sending forth to the farthest ends of the world missionaries as zealous as those who landed in Kent with Augustine, and still confronting hostile kings with the same spirit with which she confronted Attila. The number of her children is greater than in any former age. Her acquisitions in the New World have more than compensated for what she has lost in the Old. Her spiritual ascendancy extends over the vast countries which lie between the plains of the Missouri and Cape Horn, countries which a century hence, may not improbably contain a population as large as that which now inhabits Europe. The members of her communion are certainly not fewer than a hundred and fifty millions; and it will be difficult to show all other Christian sects united amount to a hundred and twenty millions. Nor do we see any sign which indicates that the term of her long dominion is approaching. She saw the commencement of all the governments and of all the ecclesiastical establishments that now exist in the world; and we feel no assurance that she is not destined to see the end of them all. She was great and respected before the Saxon had set foot on Britain, before the Frank had passed the Rhine, when Grecian eloquence still flourished at Antioch, when idols were still worshipped in the

temple of Mecca. And she may still exist in undiminished vigour when some traveller from New Zealand shall, in the midst of a vast solitude, take his stand on a broken arch of London Bridge to sketch the ruins of St Paul's.

✝ *Prayer for this Session and During the Week*

Think of one of your forebears who had an influence on your personal life or that of your family. If you knew them personally or have seen a photo of them, then spend a few minutes in prayer and thanksgiving for them.

? *For Discussion*

How can the members of the Church ensure that the message of the Gospel is preached imaginatively on television, in the press and so on?

Scripture Reading

Acts of the Apostles

For Further Reading

A History of the Church by Philip Hughes (Sheed & Ward)

The Stripping of the Altars by Eamon Duffy (Yale University Press)

Lives of the Saints by Rev. Alban Butler (Studio Editions, illustrated abridged edition)

Chapter Twenty-Four
The Church Today: Ecumenism

We have seen how there occurred a major break from the Church in the sixteenth century. This, unlike the earlier Orthodox schism, soon split up into a vast array of different 'Churches'. By 1560, sixteen years after the formation of the Church of England, the 'General Assembly' was set up in Scotland, and this, based on Calvin's teachings, gave rise to Presbyterianism. The Congregationalist Church, which more recently developed into the United Reformed Church, was started by Robert Browne in 1583, and early in the following century John Smyth in Australia instituted the Baptist Church. Then came the Quakers, and a later break-off from the Church of England were the Methodists in 1739, and, from them, a century and a quarter later, the Salvation Army. And so the sad tale of the splintering off of many other sects has gone on to the present day.

However, we are now in the Catholic Church reaping the fruits of a general council which was held in the early 1960s. It had become necessary to highlight more clearly the essentials of our Catholic faith by removing some of the unnecessary clutter accumulated over the years. A direct result of this was to appreciate better what we had in common with other Christian Churches. There is in all Churches and organisations a danger of hanging on to 'a guru's cat'.

When the guru sat down to worship each evening the ashram cat would get in the way and distract the worshippers. So he ordered that the cat be tied during evening worship.

Long after the guru died the cat continued to be tied during evening worship. And when the cat eventually died, another cat was brought to the ashram so that it could be duly tied during evening worship.

Centuries later learned treatises were written by the guru's disciples on the essential role of a cat in all properly conducted worship.

(Father de Mello)

Prayer for Unity

So, not only was the purpose of Vatican II to bring to the fore the essentials in our faith, but the Church also wished to bring closer together all those who believed in Jesus Christ. It wanted to heal the many ruptures of the past. As early as 1908, Paul Watson, who was an Anglican clergyman, had the idea of starting a week of prayer for the unity of Christians. However, by the time he had got it launched he had himself been received into the Catholic Church. A French priest, L'Abbé Coutourier, made the 'week' more universal and proposed that we prayed for the unity that God wills, through the means that he wills.

Later, various councils of Churches, on both national and local levels, were formed, and in 1990 these developed into 'Churches Together in England', with similar organisations in Ireland, Scotland and Wales. The whole ecumenical movement (ecumenism means universal, the whole Church) may be summed up in this sentence: to grow from confrontation to coexistence to co-operation to commitment to communion. Five stages, and most Churches are at present at the third or fourth stage, hopefully, gradually moving towards the final stage of 'communion'. The Catholic Church sees the sharing of Communion, in the particular sense of the Eucharist, as the end product, as it were, and not the means to that end. This, of course, gives rise to no little discussion and considerable pain.

Certain it is that we must all suffer, because the fullness of that unity for which Jesus prayed has not yet come about. At the same time, we must do all that we can to work for it, so that the followers of Christ are clear signs of God's love, and are a powerful force in a pagan world.

This is illustrated by the story of the old man who summoned his four sons to his death bed and gave each of them a thin stick. 'Now break the sticks,' he told them. This they easily did. He then got four more sticks and tied them together. 'Now try to break them,' he instructed. They were unable to. 'That's how I want you to be after my death,' he said, and he continued: 'Together and united, you will be strong.'

Taizé

With the desire on the part of so many today to bring about Christian unity, a number of communities have arisen dedicated to working for reconciliation between Christians. One of these communities is based in a tiny village in central France, Taizé; and because so many thousands of young people are involved in it, the story of how it all began is worth recounting.

In the early years of the second world war, Roger Schutz, a Lutheran theological student from Switzerland, became haunted with the idea of devoting his life to praying and working for peace and reconciliation. In his own words:

> I found myself as if impelled to do everything I could to build a community life in which reconciliation would be realised, made concrete, day by day. To begin with I must start a life of prayer alone. I would find a house where there would be prayer in the morning, at midday and in the evening and I would take in those who were fleeing, those in hiding.

He found the empty house he dreamed of in a tiny village in Burgundy, France, when he was cycling along the country lanes. He bought it and soon one or two others with a similar vision joined him. They began a life of prayer, three times a day, combined with helping refugees, mostly Jews fleeing the Nazi-occupied part of France.

By 1949 the small group of 'brothers' had committed themselves to a common life, celibacy and the sharing of goods. They used the little Romanesque village church for their daily prayer. Young people on holiday, cycling and walking stopped by, were warmly welcomed, and joined the brothers in their prayer and began talking with them about the meaning of life, who Jesus Christ is and how to be more committed to him. Each year the number of young visitors increased, and although most of them camped in the nearby fields, more space was needed for their worship together.

In 1962, this resulted in a huge new church being built by a group of Germans who wished to express in a tangible way their remorse for the atrocities of the war. The young people continued to flock to Taizé each year, thousands had to be accommodated in huts or tents, and they gathered together in the church for the thrice-daily prayer with the brothers: young people of all denominations or none, from many different countries. At least three times the church has had to be expanded by canvas awnings or more permanent wooden extensions to cater for the four to five thousand who gather there for a week at a time throughout the summer months, as well as hundreds who are to be found there even in the winter – young, and, more recently, not so young!

The community of brothers now numbers about ninety and includes many different nationalities. They work on local co-operative farms, printing, pottery, writing and suchlike. A few spend a certain time in Third World countries, and amongst them are many different Christian affiliations, including several Catholic priests.

Hengrave

Another example of prayer and work for reconciliation nearer to home is Hengrave Hall, near Bury St Edmunds, Suffolk. This is a sixteenth-century country house which was sold to the Sisters of the Assumption in 1952. (They wanted to move their community and school out of Kensington Square, London.) Thus, for the next twenty-two years, it became a boarding school for girls, until the Sisters decided that their vocation lay in a different area of the Lord's vineyard, namely, that of work for reconciliation amongst Christians. It is now an ecumenical centre for retreats and conferences, run by the community which comprises Christians of different denominations, men and women, single and married, clergy, religious and lay, long-term members and temporary volunteer helpers, also from many different countries. They live by a simple rule which commits them to a life of sharing – prayer, work, goods – together. They meet together for prayer each day. One of the principal tasks of the community is to help a new generation of Christians to become more aware of their commitment to Christ within their own Churches, and to discover a more authentic witness to the Gospel. Thus they exist as a family for others, and especially for those who are searching for a deeper meaning to life.

Non-Christian Religions

We live in a multi-faith society in Britain, and the Church reminds us that nothing of what is true and holy in other religions should be rejected. In non-Christian religions we often find teachings which 'reflect the brightness of that Truth which is the light of all men and women'. This is taken from the 'Declaration on the Relationship of the Church to Non-Christian Religions', and it goes on to say that Catholics should 'make sincere efforts at mutual understanding and... work together in protecting and promoting for the benefit of all men, social justice, good morals as well as peace and freedom.'

The Light of Christ

To conclude, it should now be clear that working for the answer to Jesus's prayer for unity, 'that they may all be one', does not mean that we want uniformity, but rather a oneness of heart and mind in centring our lives on the Risen Lord and his teaching. The Risen Christ is our Light, and as we draw closer to him through prayer and our way of life, under the guidance of the Holy Spirit, the closer we will come to one another.

There is an old Eastern story of an elephant in a dark house which appears in the book of Sufi wisdom, *The Mathnawi of Jalalu'ddin Rumi*. The story is called 'The Disagreement as to the Description and Shape of the Elephant'. In *Diagnosis of Man*, Kenneth Walker recounts the story as follows.

> The elephant was in a dark house: some Hindus had brought it for exhibition. In order to see it, many

people were going, every one, into that darkness. As seeing it with the eye was impossible, each one was feeling it in the dark with the palm of his hand.

The hand of one fell on its trunk: he said, 'This creature is like a water pipe.'

The hand of another touched its ear: to him it appeared to be like a fan. Since another handled its leg, he said, 'I found the elephant shape to be like a pillar.' Another laid his hand on the back: he said, 'Truly this elephant was like a throne.'

Similarly, when anyone heard a description of the elephant, he understood it only in respect of the part that he had touched.

If there had been a candle in each one's hand, the difference would have gone out of their words.

THE CANDLE, THE LIGHT IS CHRIST!

(For the Rite of Election, or Enrolment of names, see p.55 of the Rite.)

✝ *Prayer for this Session and During the Week*

Listen to a tape of Taizé chants.

Lord Jesus, your sign of reconciliation is the cross in all its breadth and length and height and depth.
Teach us to share it with you and our sisters and brothers
so that we may learn to act justly, to walk humbly, to love tenderly.
And so, waiting upon the Spirit, become instruments of Your peace to the glory of
the Father. Amen.

(The Hengrave Prayer)

The light of Christ has come into the world
the light of Christ has come into the world.

All men must be born again
to see the kingdom of God
the water the Spirit
bring new life in God's love.

God gave up his only Son
out of love for the world

so that ev'ryone who believes in him
will live forever.

The Light of God has come to us
so that we might have salvation,
from the darkness of our sins, we walk
into the glory with Christ Jesus.

(Donald Fishel, 1974, *The Word of God*)

? *For Discussion*

What are the obstacles in your area to a deeper understanding between Christians of different Churches?

What could and should Catholics sacrifice (give up) in the cause of unity?

Scripture Reading

John 17

For Further Reading

Any books about Taizé, but especially *A Universal Heart* by Kathryn Spink (SPCK)

'Declaration on the Relationship of the Church to Non-Christian Religions' (CTS Do.360)

THE DESSERT

Lenten Period

Chapter Twenty-Five
Lent: Reflecting on the Past and Looking Forward to Easter
(First Week of Lent)

Lent begins on Ash Wednesday, and the sessions during Lent take the form of a more spiritual and immediate preparation for baptism or reception into the Church at the Easter Vigil. However, in the first week of Lent it is good to reflect on the past instructional sessions to see how you feel about them generally. Suggestions are given for the other weeks of Lent, but with the specific instruction sessions completed it is mainly a time when there is freedom to think and pray and ponder. Some may find the six talks by Father Anthony de Mello on 'A Way to God for Today' on video to be useful. They comprise six half-hour talks, followed by practical prayer exercises.

Usually around the first Sunday of Lent there takes place what is known as the Rite of Election. This is held in the cathedral of the diocese and all who have taken part in the journey in faith, together with their sponsors, are invited to go. It is designed to mark the fact that those who are to be received into the Church at Easter 'have undergone a conversion in mind and in action, and have developed a sufficient acquaintance with Christian teaching as well as a spirit of faith and charity' (The Rite of Christian Initiation of Adults, p.55). Father de Mello sums it up in this way:

The Master's sermon that day consisted of only one enigmatic sentence.

He just gave a wry smile and began, 'All I do here is sit by the bank of the river selling river water.'

And with that he ended his sermon.

He had set up his stall on the river-bank, this water-seller, and thousands came to buy water from him. The whole success of his trade depended on their not seeing the river. When they finally saw it, he ran out of business.

'Unless I go,' said Jesus, 'the Holy Spirit will not come.'

✝ *Prayer for this Session and During the Week*

Be aware of yourself: the sensations in your body;
be aware of the sounds around you;
be aware of your breathing.
Thank God for the various parts of your body.
Thank God for all that you recall of the sessions we have had together.

? *For Discussion*

What have you found most useful in these instructional sessions?

Scripture Reading

Deuteronomy 26:4–10
Romans 10:8–13
Luke 4:1–13
These are all readings for the Rite of Election.

For Further Reading

The Catechism of the Catholic Church (Geoffrey Chapman)

Chapter Twenty-Six
Faith in and Devotion to the Bread of Life
(Second Week of Lent)

Father René Voillaume, the founder of the Little Brothers of Charles de Foucauld, whose spirituality centres very much on the Presence of Jesus in the Eucharist, sums up what our faith in this Bread of Life means to us – this could be read as a prolonged meditation.

> The Eucharist is a baffling mystery for human reason. When we consider that uninterruptedly, throughout the entire Christian Church, for the last two thousand years, bread and wine have been consecrated and offered as the Saviour commanded in memory of him, we are not faced with an abstraction but with a prodigiously concrete reality: the reality of bread and wine. What Christ intended, by founding, by creating, the Eucharist, he and he alone can tell us.
>
> What Christ himself did on the eve of his death, and what has been done since, over and over again, innumerable times, by virtue of the power that he himself conferred, is truly one and the same thing. Whether done by Jesus, or by the priests instituted by him, it is always the same Eucharist, it always will be

the same. It will endure century after century, until the end of the world.

The type of bread may change, the type of wine may change, the accompanying prayers may change, but the words pronounced by Christ will not change, and the Eucharist will be what Christ made it; men have no power over it; no one can debase it.

Here then we find a very clear, a very concrete reality, which we can see, which we can touch, which we can eat, but the true nature of which we can only grasp by faith in the words of Christ. This then is a true example of what faith is, since nothing is visible to the eye, nothing is verifiable by experiment, everything is of the order of the invisible. It is a reality which faith alone can reveal to us. Were we to run through the history of the varying forms of Eucharistic celebration, or of the endless speculations of Catholic or non-Catholic theologians who have attempted to understand and define what the Eucharist is, this would fall short of the necessary act of faith and we should none of us be any the wiser...

There are indeed a number of different aspects to be grasped. Besides the relationship with the Passion and death of Jesus, introducing the idea of the sacrifice of the New Covenant, there is also the idea of food, wonderfully expressed by Jesus himself in his discourse on the bread of life (see John 6:26–59). Then again there is that aspect of the Eucharist as being given to the Church, as principle and expression of the Church's unity.

All these aspects were affirmed by Christ himself, as also by Saint Paul. But these various functions of the Eucharist, as sacrifice, as food and as sacrament of unity, together presuppose that Christ is truly though mysteriously present with his body and with his blood in the consecrated bread and wine. It seems best, therefore, to begin with this notion of the presence of Christ in the Eucharist, which has given rise in time past as also today, to so many controversies, debates and efforts to explain what this really means.

You remember Christ's words over the bread: 'This is my body'. They are simple words, words that could not be simpler. There is a subject, a verb of affirmation and a complement.

If we now turn to the discourse on the bread of life recorded by Saint John, we cannot help being struck by the force and realism used by Jesus there too. It is one of his most remarkable discourses.

In it, Christ offers himself to mankind as food, as bread come down from heaven, as the bread given by God himself. At the outset, we understand Christ to be the bread of life because he is the Word of God: he feeds us with his truth and with his teaching. But by an imperceptible transition, Jesus then passes on to the Eucharist. And here his discourse acquires a nearly shocking realism: 'He who eats my flesh and drinks my blood has eternal life'. And he repeats the same statement several times, as though afraid of not being understood – so often indeed that the listening Jews were horrified. To understand their sense of outrage and how at the same time their sense of outrage underlines the objective, realist character of the Lord's words, we have to put ourselves in those Jews' place as they listened to him talking of eating the flesh of the Son of Man, and above all of drinking his blood...

Christ is now living in the glory of the Father – a non-terrestrial life – and hence his presence can never take a terrestrial form. Each and every one of the hosts consecrated throughout the world is related to the presence of Christ, without Christ being either changed or multiplied.

That magnificent Latin hymn 'Adoro te devote' admirably states the orthodox faith: it says that neither sight, nor taste, nor touch can detect the presence of Christ; but only, among five senses, hearing leads us into the heart of the mystery, by allowing us to hear Christ's words: 'This is my body', and so to adhere to them by faith: and this faith makes it possible for us to share Christ's own understanding of the mystery that he himself has instituted.

Thus in a world far beyond the senses is where we have to site the Eucharist and take our part in it, not that the Lord may not occasionally grant us feelings of joy, of fulfilment, of certitude, known as sensible graces.

And now, to speak of the Eucharist as sacrifice – since this above all was the reason why Christ instituted the Eucharist. We affirm that by this presence and by the consecration at Mass, we are brought into relationship with the sacrifice on the Cross. This is an aspect of the Eucharist sacrifice which is frequently under-emphasised, although the very words of consecration declare it by using the words of the Lord himself: 'Do this in memory of me'. And the Apostle Paul is even more explicit: 'Until the Lord comes, therefore, every time you eat this bread and drink this cup, you are proclaiming his death...' (1 Corinthians 11:26)

We proclaim his passion; and by communion we are united to the sacrifice of Christ and share in its fruits.

I have already mentioned that the Christian life consists in reliving the mystery of Christ. By the same token, we have also to relive his passion and his death on the Cross, and this is what gives a hidden and almost infinite dimension to our sufferings, to our troubles, as well as the quality of participating, in the name of mankind, in all suffering.

One of the fruits of communion in the Eucharistic sacrifice should be precisely this: to help us to live this particular truth.

The Eucharistic sacrifice is also the pre-eminent sacrifice of praise. For Christ's offering of himself is now consummated in the eternal glory of the Resurrected Lord eternally praising his Father, and of this praise the offering of the Eucharistic sacrifice is the highest form. We too have our part in this praise.

I need not perhaps insist on the aspect of the Eucharist as communion. In this sacrament, we communicate truly with the Body and Blood of Christ as with the food of life, and this is bestowed on us when we take our part in the sacrifice from which this food derives its life-giving power.

Since Christ is forever interceding with the Father, Christ's prayer is also truly present with him in the Sacrament. This permanence of Christ as prayer in the Eucharist we recognise and show forth by the continual reservation of the Sacrament in church or in Christian communities, as a constant invitation for us to unite ourselves at all times to the Lord's own adoration and intercession...

We ought to regard the Eucharist as an inestimable treasure. How amazing it is, once you start thinking about it! The Church could have got rid of the Eucharist centuries ago! Considering all the heresies, all the attacks, all the minimising interpretations of which the Eucharist has been the object: it would have sufficed to cease celebrating it, or to cease consecrating priests, and that would have been the end of it. Yet Christians of all traditions despite the strife, despite the clash of doctrine, have always retained the Eucharistic celebration. People may argue about it, but it is always there, an irrefutable and abiding sign of the Son of Man's incomprehensible love for his fellow men.

(*Faith and Contemplation,*
Père René Voillaume, pp.70–78)

The outward forms of devotion to and recognition of the Lord's Presence in the Eucharist have varied over the ages. Lent provides a good opportunity to think and pray about your attitude to the Eucharist, and to grow in faith and love of the Blessed Sacrament.

On a practical note, you could be considering how you are hoping to receive Holy Communion when you are received into the Church – under both kinds, in the hand or mouth and so on. Furthermore, how will you, in the secret of your heart, respond in love to Jesus's Presence within you in those moments of stillness after you have received Holy Communion?

✞ *Prayer for this Session and During the Week*

Make a prolonged visit to the Blessed Sacrament, preferably when there is nothing going on in the church.

🕮 *Scripture Reading*

Read again the whole of chapter six of John's Gospel.

🕮 *For Further Reading*

Christian Vocation by René Voillaume (DLT)

Chapter Twenty-Seven
Confession
(Third Week of Lent)

Earlier we saw something of the nature of sin and the way the sacrament of reconciliation (confession) has developed over the ages. Now we need to see how to 'go to confession'. First of all it must be said that probably no one likes going to confession. It can never be pleasant telling the Lord, in the presence of someone else, the priest, in what ways we have acted wrongly. However, the peace and joy experienced after making a good confession and knowing that we have been welcomed back to the Father's house (refer again to the parable of the 'The Prodigal Son'), is truly a cause for gratitude and praise and celebration.

Before Confession

Prior to going to see the priest for confession, it is important to do three things:

- Ask God, through his Holy Spirit, to help and guide you.
- Read a passage from Scripture. Encountering God's word should help us to realise to what extent we have failed to live up to it.
- Ponder on your personal sins and failings. Without making a shopping list of them, think in what ways you

have failed in love of God, your neighbour and yourself. Then there is the whole issue of social sin, being caught up in the evils of our society, living according to standards which cause others to lose their freedom and become underprivileged. An area sometimes worth looking at is the way in which our most frequent faults are linked with the sort of character we have ('Am I basically a lazy person, an 'activist', an angry person?' And if so, 'Why?'), or the way of life we lead.

In Confession

The priest may be available at certain advertised times in the confessional 'box' or room, in which case the penitent waits their turn – if there are others there – before entering, then closing the door and kneeling to speak through the grille, or, if there is a choice, sitting for a 'face-to-face' confession. Alternatively, you may have made a specific appointment to see the priest. It is usual to begin by introducing yourself (unless it is a face-to-face confession and the priest already knows you quite well) in a general sort of way: not by name, but by stating simply, for example, that you are a college student, a mother with nineteen children or that you have been recently widowed. It is also usual to mention roughly how long it has been since your last confession, before proceeding to talk about your sins and failings. Inevitably, with a face-to-face confession there is less formality. However, if it is through the grille, it is as well to indicate that you have finished by adding words to the effect that, 'For these and all the other things I cannot now remember, I am truly sorry.'

The priest will then probably give you some advice, tell you what your penance is (for example, to pray in some particular way or to perform some small act of kindness), ask you to tell God you are truly sorry ('an act of contrition', either in some set form, or in your own words; for example, 'Lord, I am sorry for all that I have confessed, all that I cannot now remember, and I will try to do better in the future'), and then pronounce God's forgiveness (the words of absolution, during which, if it is face-to-face, he may extend his hands over you).

After Confession

It is then good to leave the confessional and spend a while in thanksgiving to God for the love and peace he gives you through this sacrament.

First Confession

For your first confession it is very normal to be a little apprehensive, although you need not be! It is certainly best to make this as informal as possible, and so face-to-face and to a priest who knows you is preferable. However, as has already been mentioned, this is your choice. Clearly, on reflecting on your failings over the years you will recall only some of them, and you are advised to confess your general and frequent 'falls' together with those matters that stand out in your mind. Remember that it is the Lord who hears you and he is always loving and merciful and understanding. 'Fear not!'

The 'scrutinies', which are usually celebrated on the third, fourth and fifth Sundays of Lent are rites of self-searching and repentance, and are followed by the presentation of the Creed and The Lord's Prayer. All this may be adapted according to the particular needs and situation of the group, the individual and the parish. (For the Rites during Lent, see p.69 of the Rite.)

Thus Lent is a good time to examine our 'baobabs', as described in this extract from Saint Exupery's *The Little Prince*.

A baobab is something you will never, never be able to get rid of if you attend to it too late. It spreads over the entire planet. It bores clear through it with its roots. And if the planet is too small, and the baobabs are too many, they split it in pieces...

'It is a question of discipline,' the little prince said to me later on. 'When you've finished your own toilet in the morning, then it is time to attend to the toilet of your planet, just so, with the greatest care. You must see to it that you pull up regularly all the baobabs, at the very first moment when they can be distinguished from the rose bushes which they resemble so closely in their earliest youth. It is very tedious work,' the little prince added, 'but very easy.'

And one day he said to me: 'You ought to make a beautiful drawing, so that the children where you live can see exactly how all this is. That would be very useful to them if they were to travel some day. Sometimes,' he added, 'there is no harm in putting off a piece of work until another day. But when it is a matter of baobabs, that always means a catastrophe. I knew a planet that was inhabited by a lazy man. He neglected three little bushes...

So, as the little prince described it to me, I have made a drawing of that planet. I do not much like to take the tone of a moralist. But the danger of the baobabs is so little understood, and such considerable risks would be run by anyone who might get lost on an asteroid, that for once I am breaking through my reserve. 'Children,' I say plainly, 'watch out for the baobabs!'

My friends, like myself, have been skirting this danger for a long time, without ever knowing it; and so it is for them that I have worked so hard over this drawing. The lesson which I pass on by this means is worth all the trouble it has cost me.

Yes, we all have a baobab at varying stages of growth – a fault or failing or sin that needs rooting out before it overruns our whole being – and the Lord, in the sacrament of reconciliation, helps us to do just this.

✠ *Prayer for this Session and During the Week*

An act of contrition:

O God, I am sorry and ask forgiveness for my sins.
By the help of your grace I will try not to sin again.

? *For Discussion*

What do you think you will find most difficult about going to confession? Why?

It can be both helpful and amusing for a priest and a lay person to 'act out' (role-play) a mock confession, both 'in the box', and 'face-to-face', and follow it with discussion.

Scripture Reading

Luke 6:27–38
Colossians 3:5–17

For Further Reading

Re-read chapter seventeen of this book on the sacrament of reconciliation

A Simple Penance Book (CTS)

Chapter Twenty-Eight
Coming In
(Fourth Week of Lent)

At this stage, if not before, most people have doubts and hesitations rearing their heads. These can be for many reasons. Vernon Johnson, an Anglican priest who became a Catholic in the early part of the century, said that he delayed entering the Church for some time:

> I am just a very ordinary Englishman; and as such, I had within me, bred in my very bones, all the dread and fear and suspicion of Rome, and the distrust of what I considered ecclesiastical intrigue and Italian government – the latent hostility which I had inherited as part of the normal English education and tradition – all this I had to a quite extraordinary degree.
>
> (*One Lord One Faith*, Vernon Johnson, Sheed & Ward, 1929)

Father Clarke, the priest who received Group Captain Leonard Cheshire into the Church, wrote:

> Your submission to the Church does not imply in any way a denial of the graces you have received hitherto in your life. Catholicism is essentially a positive thing and refuses to deny the existence of

> truth in other religions, however defective they may be. Christ is the fulfilment of all partial truths and Catholicism can do no less than imitate its founder, and so your act of submission only brings to fulfilment and perfection all your religious experience that has gone before.
>
> (*The Face of Victory*
> Leonard Cheshire, VC, 1961)

Perhaps the most reassuring testimony comes from Janet Erskine Stuart. Janet was the daughter of an Anglican bishop, and in 1879 became interested in Catholicism. She started having instructions with a Jesuit, Father Gallway, but her father was strongly opposed to the step she was proposing to take, and got her to go to see Mr Gladstone, the prime minister, for whom she had great respect. Gladstone tried to dissuade her, and she finally went back to Father Gallway, as she felt that unless he could remove the doubts and fears which had been aroused by the visit to Gladstone, she could never become a Catholic. She recounts:

> I said to Father Gallway: 'Supposing I don't find my mind satisfied, once I have been received into the Church, I shall have put my neck in a noose quite unnecessarily.' Father Gallway was sympathetic, and entertained the idea seriously. After a moment he said thoughtfully: 'I really don't see that you will be so much worse off than you are now, you will only have to go a stage further on and seek the truth elsewhere.' This was far more reassuring to me than any discourse of the blessedness of the faith, and the impossibility of being dissatisfied when one was once in possession of it.

Janet was received into the Church shortly after this. She later became a nun in the Sacred Heart congregation at Wimbledon, giving up her great love of 'the good life', and in particular of travel. Time passed and she became Superior of the community and then Superior General of the whole worldwide congregation. In this role she had to travel around to visit the various convents throughout the world. '...set your hearts on his kingdom,' said Jesus, 'and these other things will be given you as well.' (Luke 12:31)

St Paul expresses it in this way:

> Not that I have secured it already, not yet reached my goal, but I am still pursuing it in the attempt to take hold of the prize for which Christ Jesus took hold of me. Brothers, I do not reckon myself as having taken hold of it; I can only say that forgetting all that lies behind me, and straining forward to what lies in front, I am racing towards the finishing-point to win the prize of God's heavenly call in Christ Jesus. So this is the way in which all of us who are mature should be thinking, and if you are still thinking differently in any way, then God has yet to make this matter clear to you. Meanwhile, let us go forward from the point we have each attained.
>
> (Phil 3:12–16)

FINISH

Prayer for this Session and During the Week

PRAYER OF ABANDONMENT OF CHARLES DE FOUCAULD

Father, I abandon myself into your hands;
do with me what you will.
Whatever you may do, I thank you;
I am ready for all, I accept all.
Let only your will be done in me,
and in all your creatures.
I wish no more than this, O Lord.
Into your hands I commend my soul;
I offer it you with all the love of my heart,
for I love you Lord, and so need to give myself,
to surrender myself into your hands, without reserve,
and with boundless confidence, for you are my Father.

For Discussion

Pick out one or two of the different forms of prayer that have been highlighted over the past weeks. Talk about them – and perhaps pray them again.

Scripture Reading

Acts 22:1–21

For Further Reading

No Man Is an Island by Thomas Merton

Chapter Twenty-Nine
Retreat
(Fifth Week of Lent)

This could be an evening retreat, or, preferably, extend to half a day or a whole day. It could, depending on circumstances, take place in the parish church, or, if possible, in a religious house, a convent or monastery or quiet place not too far away. Normally, it would be led by a priest or retreat-giver.

Silence and plenty of time for reflection are important. Suitable taped background music may be used for a little of the time, perhaps at the beginning. A suitable reading could be John 3, the story of the conversion of Nicodemus, or perhaps the whole of St Paul's letter to the Ephesians. It would be good, too, to reflect on the 'journey' so far and on the readings and prayers of the forthcoming Easter Vigil, when you will be baptised or received into full communion with the Catholic Church.

Chapter Thirty
The Easter Vigil
(Sixth Week of Lent)

Reception into the Church normally takes place in the course of the Easter Vigil and the first Mass of Easter. It is appropriate this week to spend some time reading through the liturgy of the Vigil Service and Mass. It is rich in symbolism – fire, light, water, oil, bread and wine – as well as including in the readings an outline of the way God chose and led his people up to the coming of Christ.

To Ponder On

> Do not look forward to what might happen tomorrow; the same everlasting Father who cares for you today, will take care of you tomorrow and every day. Either he will shield you from suffering or he will give you unfailing strength to bear it. Be at peace then, and put aside all anxious thoughts and imaginings.
>
> (St Francis de Sales)

> ...be light-hearted and contented, because you are called to be a member of Christ's pilgrim church. Realise the paradox of making merry and rejoicing in the world because it is not yours.
>
> (Origin Unknown)

THE COCONUT

A monkey on a tree hurled a coconut at the head of a Sufi.

The man picked it up, drank the milk, ate the flesh and made a bowl from the shell.

(Father de Mello)

THE GRACE

May the grace of our Lord Jesus Christ,
the love of God
and the fellowship of the Holy Spirit, be with us all,
now, and for evermore. Amen.

THE COFFEE
Eastertide

Chapter Thirty-One
Preparing for Pentecost and After

Through baptism and reception into the Catholic Church, the convert has become an important and unique member of Christ's Body. At the first session after Easter it is good to reflect on and share the experience of the Easter Vigil. The catechist or sponsor will help in the process of digestion and assimilation, and during these seven weeks leading up to the feast of Pentecost, other members of the parish will share their experiences of being part of the Church. Baptism, or being received into full communion of the Church, is never just an individual act. It is always an act by which a person shares in the whole life of Christ and of all his people: it is a belonging.

Whatever form one's spiritual life takes on, it must be clearly based on time given to communion with the Lord in prayer, regularly, and, if possible, daily. We have seen some of the different forms that prayer can take. Time given to personal prayer is the basis of any activity we may engage upon in the context of the Church's life and the fulfilment of our baptismal promises.

It may well be that the new member of the Church wants more time to learn and assimilate, and will in no way wish to rush into any Church involvement. Some may wish to follow some of the sessions again, and perhaps take part in welcoming others about to make the journey in faith. In some places the new member of the Church shares their faith story, not only with those in the following year's group, but also in the context of the parish Sunday liturgy. However, for most, the latter might well be too daunting!

No details of these sessions are given, as they will vary from place to place. However, mostly, the seven weeks between reception into the Church at Easter and the celebration of Mass, usually with the bishop of the diocese, at Pentecost, will comprise a number of sessions at which members of different parish or town groups will talk about their various activities. These groups may be 'home-grown' parish groups, for example:

- House groups.
- Prayer groups.
- Bible study groups.

Or they may be linked to a national or international organisation, for example:

- The Society of St Vincent de Paul (to help the poor and the lonely).
- The Legion of Mary (engaged in parish visiting, and various forms of parish work).
- The Catholic Women's League.
- The Union of Catholic Mothers.
- Teams of Our Lady (for married couples).
- Justice & Peace groups (local and Third World interests).

Then there are various activities connected with the liturgy (the various ministries of reader, welcomer, the Eucharist and so on) and the general running of the parish. Some people thrive and grow in the context of a group, whilst others would fight shy of this, but feel they could be useful as individuals doing a more solitary task, such as typing, helping with the accounts, working in the sacristy or being a general 'handyman'.

This, then, is a time to hear, first-hand, about all this, and perhaps, after further thought and prayer, become involved in the building up of Christ's Kingdom in one or other of these ways.

Thus the newly incorporated member of the Church should not only continue to be formed and moulded by the parish community, but he or she should also contribute to the community. Raymond Kemp concludes his book, *A Journey in Faith*, written in the early days of the restoration of the Rite of Christian Initiation for Adults, with these words:

> The neophytes add more than an impetus to the evangelical nature of the Easter event. They crystallise in new and fresh ways the experience of salvation. Part of our problem as Catholics has been an ethereal definition of salvation and redemption. We have heard the words so often that we have come to equate them with heaven. How surprised we are when the person in the next pew says that salvation means a complete change in the way he or she approaches life. When the garden club is replaced by scripture study, when the donation to charity becomes an afterthought to the service to be performed for the one in need in front of you, then the definition of salvation begins to take a more earthly form. When persons who used to fear strangers and never would let anyone get too close are now ready to endure the possibility of being hurt in opening themselves to one another, then salvation comes down to earth. When the owner of cupboards full of

> clothes and the latest model car can say that people are more important than things and he is ready to volunteer two nights a week in youth work, then salvation becomes flesh and blood.
>
> We do what we do because of Easter. And because of Easter we encourage one another to keep doing for the sake of a new creation.

This little book (like a number of others on similar lines), can be recommended for catechists, sponsors and others involved in guiding those who are making the journey in faith.

In the Catechism of the Catholic Church (p.209) we find a quotation from Vatican II, followed by a paragraph which makes this very clear.

> Lay believers are in the front line of Church life; for them the Church is the animating principle of human society. Therefore, they in particular ought to have an ever-clearer consciousness not only of belonging to the Church, but of being the Church, that is to say, the community of the faithful on earth under the leadership of the Pope, the common Head, and of the bishops in communion with him. They are the Church.
>
> Since, like all the faithful, lay Christians are entrusted by God with the apostolate by virtue of the Baptism and Confirmation, they have the right and duty, individually or grouped in associations, to work so that the divine message of salvation may be known and accepted by all men throughout the earth. The duty is the more pressing when it is only through them that men can hear the Gospel and know Christ. Their activity in ecclesial communities is so necessary

> that, for the most part, the apostolate of the pastors cannot be fully effective without it.

Remember that each one is unique and is called by the Lord in a slightly different way. Each one's faith and love and hope is important for the building up of Christ's Church, and the spread of his Kingdom. Think about the following story.

THE WEIGHT OF NOTHING

'Tell me the weight of a snowflake,' a coalmouse asked a wild dove.

'Nothing more than nothing,' was the answer.

'In that case I must tell you a marvellous story,' the coalmouse said. 'I sat on the branch of a fir, close to its trunk, when it began to snow, not heavily, not in a raging blizzard, no, just like in a dream, without any violence. Since I didn't have anything better to do, I counted the snowflakes settling on the twigs and needles of my branch. Their number was exactly 3,741,952. When the next snowflake dropped on to the branch – nothing more than nothing, as you say – the branch broke off.'

Having said that, the coalmouse flew away.

The dove, since Noah's time an authority on the matter, thought about the story for a while and finally said to herself: 'Perhaps there is only one person's voice lacking for peace to come about in the world... perhaps there is only one person's faith lacking for the world to be changed.'

(Origin Unknown)

Conclusion

We begin life with nothing, and we end our lives with nothing. Everything on the journey between these two moments is borrowed: given to us for our use by God. Provided we have the essentials, then the happier we are. The most joyful people I have ever met were destitute and homeless people being cared for by the Missionaries of the Poor in Jamaica. They had nothing – and yet they had everything. God's love was being showered on them through the work of the Brothers.

It is this concern and love that enables us to grow; and it is our loving response to God's love that becomes an essential part of us, and that we take with us to the next life.

May the journey in faith be accompanied by the journey in love and hope.

> Lord God, Light of the minds that know you, Life of the souls that love you, and Strength of the thoughts that seek you, help us so to know you that we may truly love you, and so to love you that we may fully serve you, whose service is perfect freedom; through Jesus Christ our Lord.
>
> (Gelasian Sacramentary)